SPECTRUM®

Spelling

Grade K

Published by Spectrum®
an imprint of Carson-Dellosa Publishing LLC
Greensboro, NC

Spectrum® is an imprint of Carson-Dellosa Publishing.

Send all inquiries to:
Carson-Dellosa Publishing
P.O. Box 35665
Greensboro, NC 27425

Printed in the USA

ISBN 978-0-7696-8010-1

02-366127811

Table of Contents Grade K

Table of Contents, continued

ABC Chart

Aa Bb Cc Dd

Ee Ff Gg Hh

Ii Jj Kk Ll Mm

Nn Oo Pp Qq

Rr Ss Tt Uu Vv

Ww Xx Yy Zz

NAME ______________________

Lesson 1 The Letters **I, L, T, K**

Say the letter **I**. Trace it. Write it on the line.

I i

Circle the letter **i** in each word.

igloo

tire

ice cream

bib

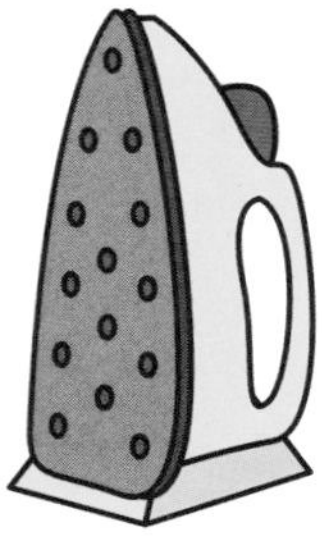

iron

wig

NAME ____________________________

Lesson 1 The Letters **I**, **L**, **T**, **K**

Say the letter **L**. Trace it. Write it on the line.

Follow the letters **L** and **l** to help the lamb find its mom.

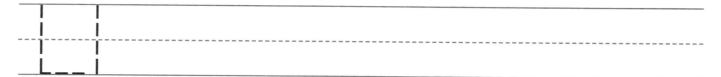

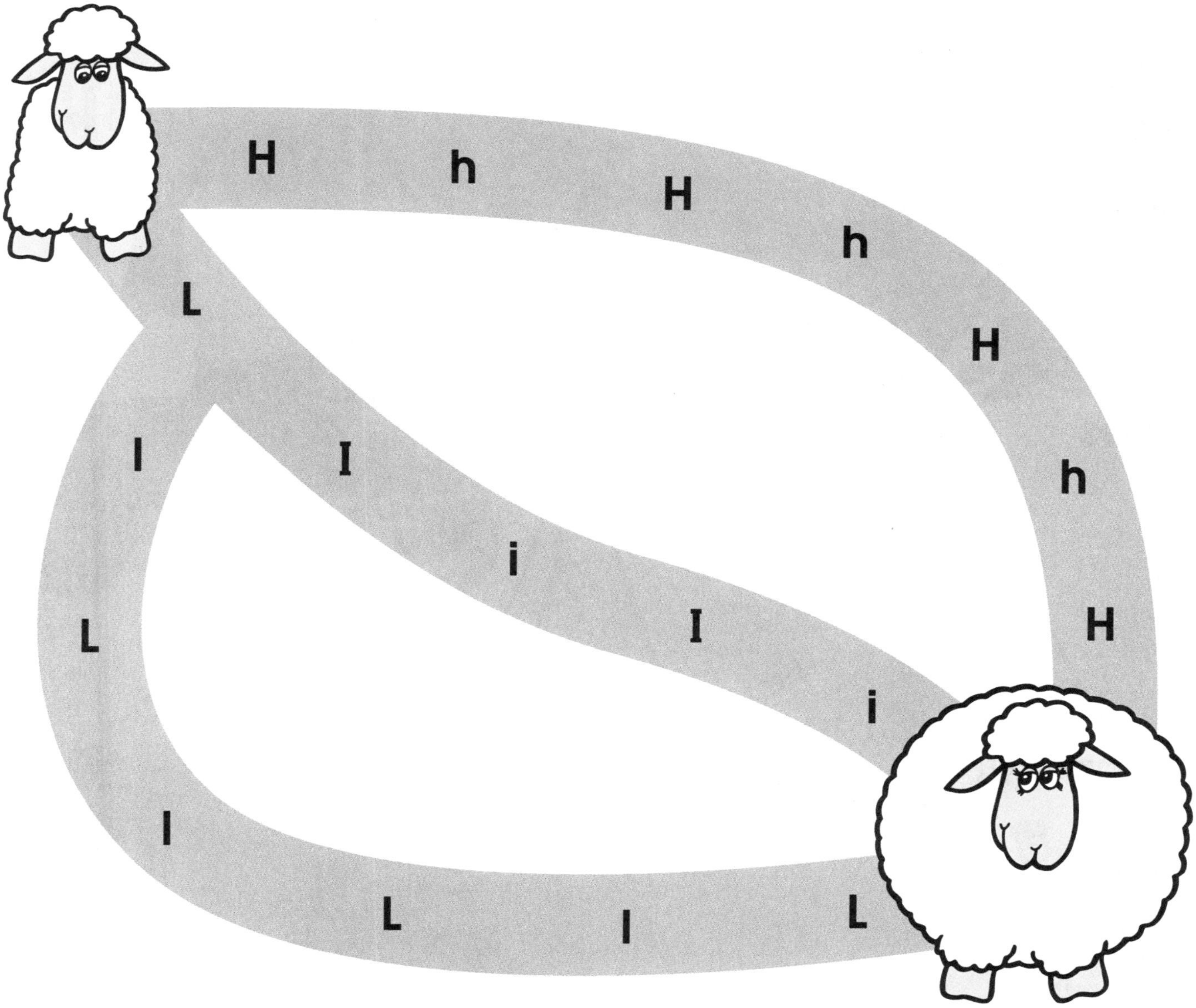

NAME ______________________

Lesson 1 The Letters I, L, T, K

Say the letter **T**. Trace it. Write it on the line.

Circle the letter **t** in each word.

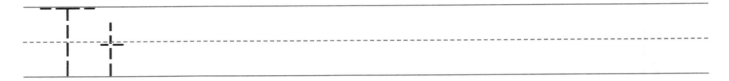

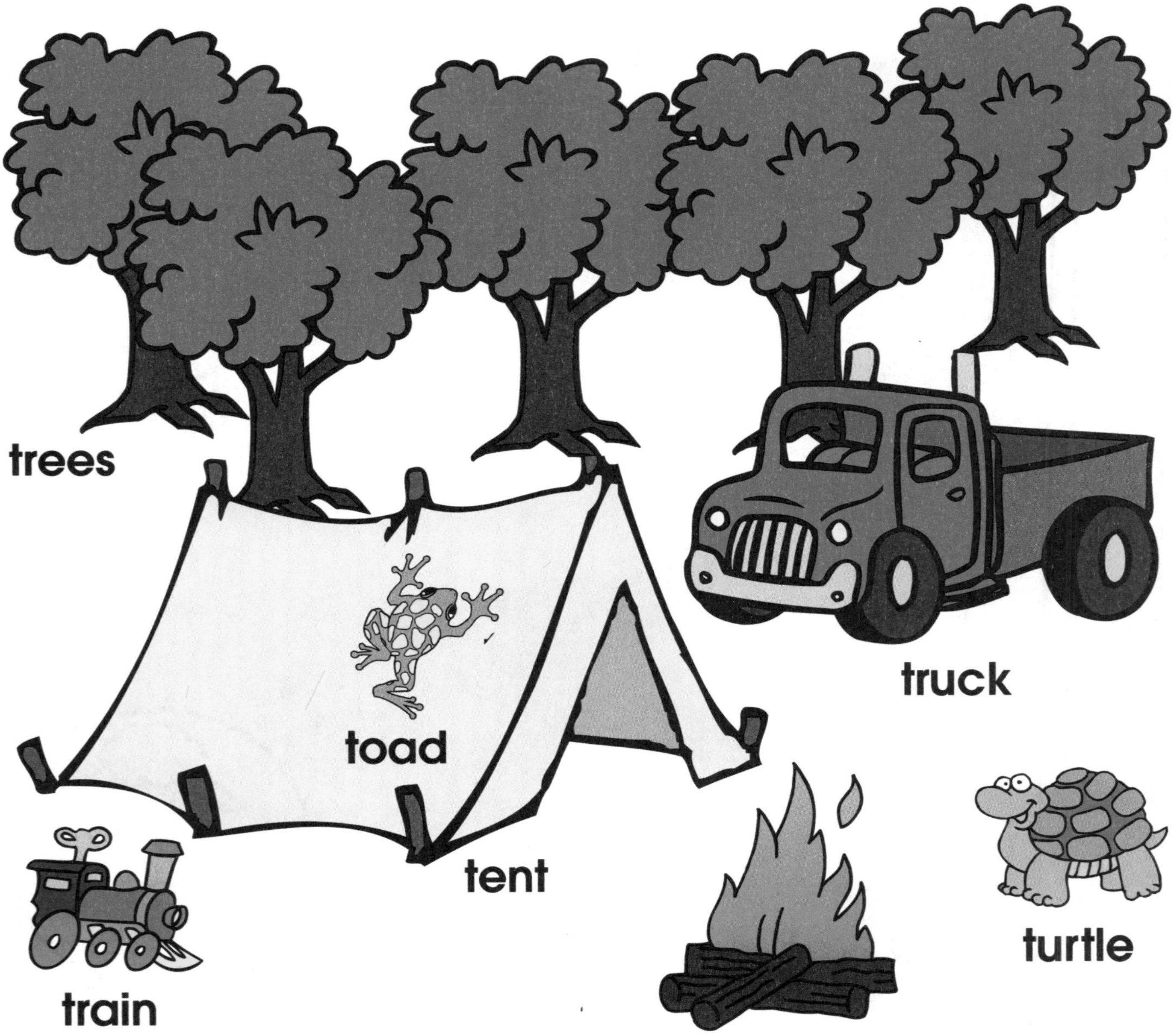

NAME ______________________________

Lesson 1 The Letters **I**, **L**, **T**, **K**

Say the letter **K**. Trace it. Write it on the line.

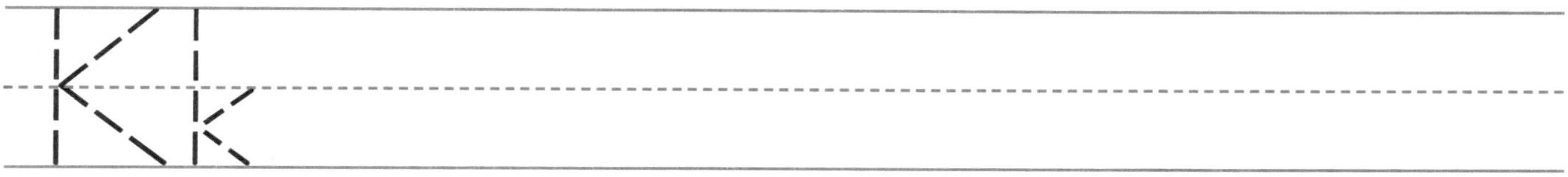

Color the kites with a capital **K** orange. Color the kites with a lowercase **k** blue.

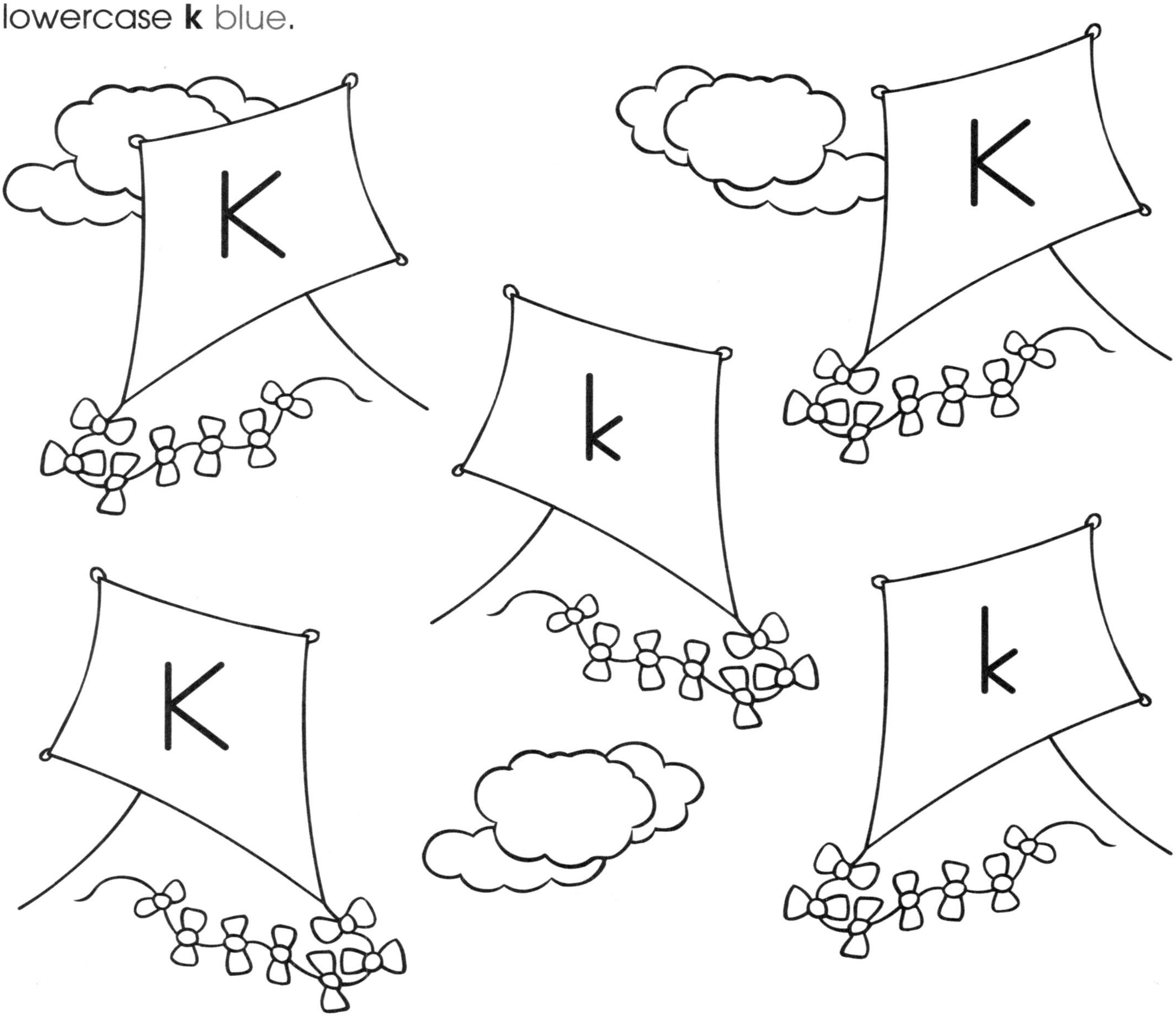

NAME ______________________

Lesson 2 The Letters **Y, Z, V, W, X**

Say the letter **Y**. Trace it. Write it on the line.

Y y

Say the letter **Z**. Trace it. Write it on the line.

Z z

Find the hidden picture. Color the spaces with **Yy** or **Zz**.

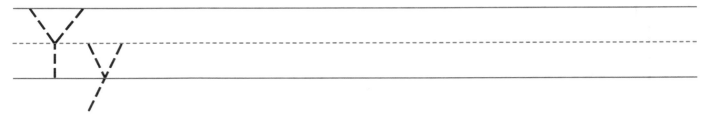

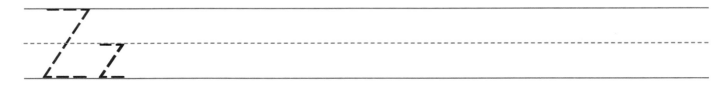

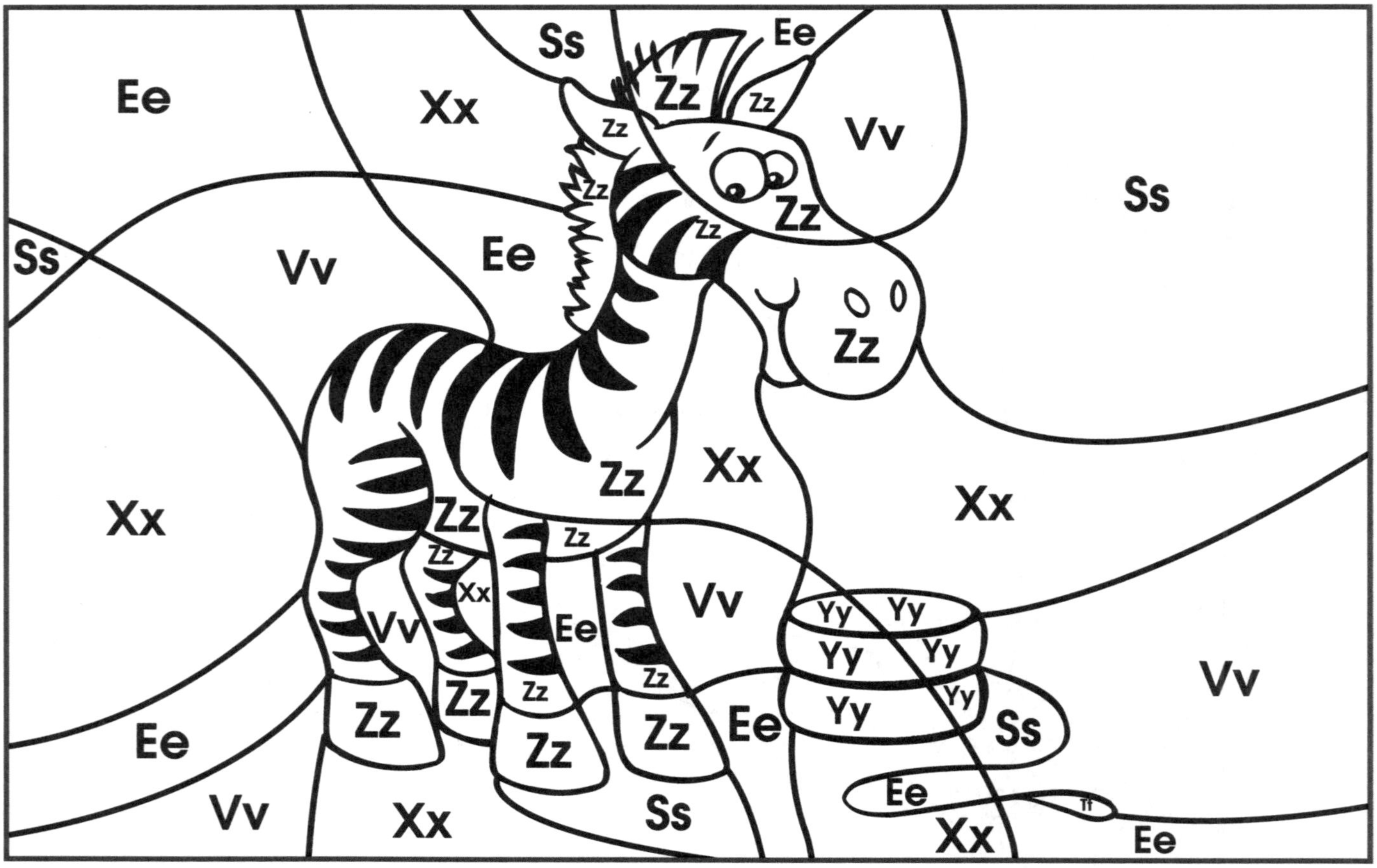

Lesson 2 The Letters **Y, Z, V, W, X**

Say the letter **V**. Trace it. Write it on the line.

V v

Write a capital **V** on the yellow vans. Write a lowercase **v** on the green vans.

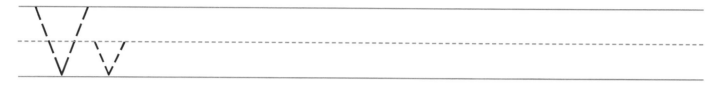

NAME ______________________________

Lesson 2 The Letters **Y**, **Z**, **V**, **W**, **X**

Say the letter **W**. Trace it. Write it on the line.

W w

Say each word. Write the missing letter **w** on the line.

___ig

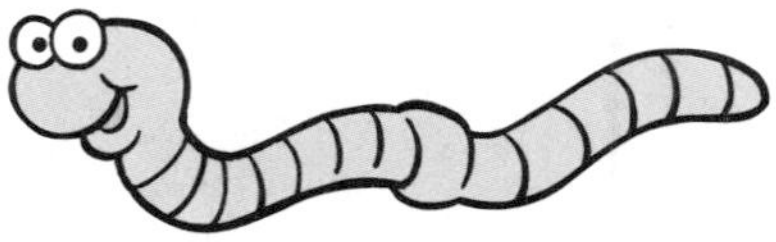

___orm

___hale

___eb

___ing

___atch

NAME ______________________

Lesson 2 The Letters **Y, Z, V, W, X**

Say the letter **X**. Trace it. Write it on the line.

Circle the letter **x** in each word.

fox

ax

six

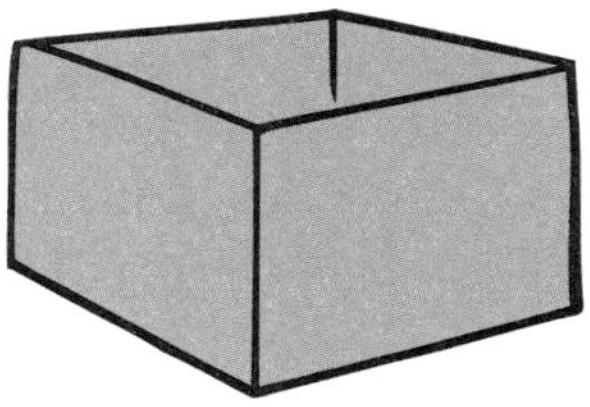

box

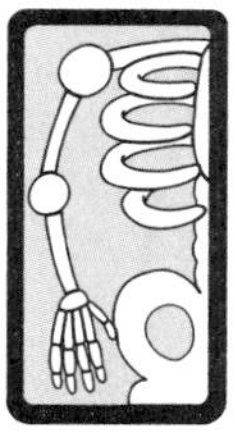

X-ray

ox

Lesson 3 The Letters **O, C, U, S**

Say the letter **O**. Trace it. Write it on the line.

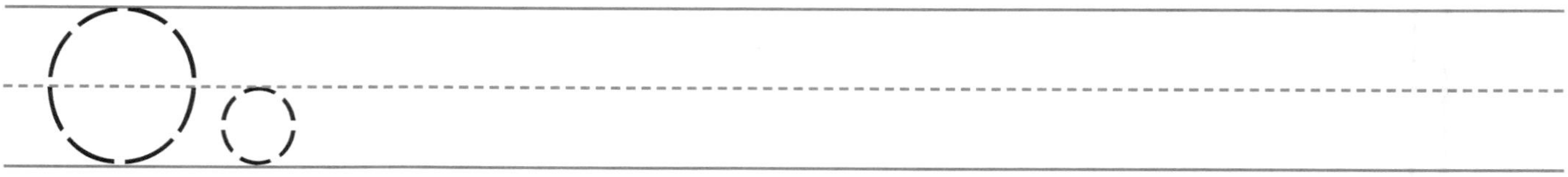

Find the hidden picture. Color the spaces with **O** or **o**.

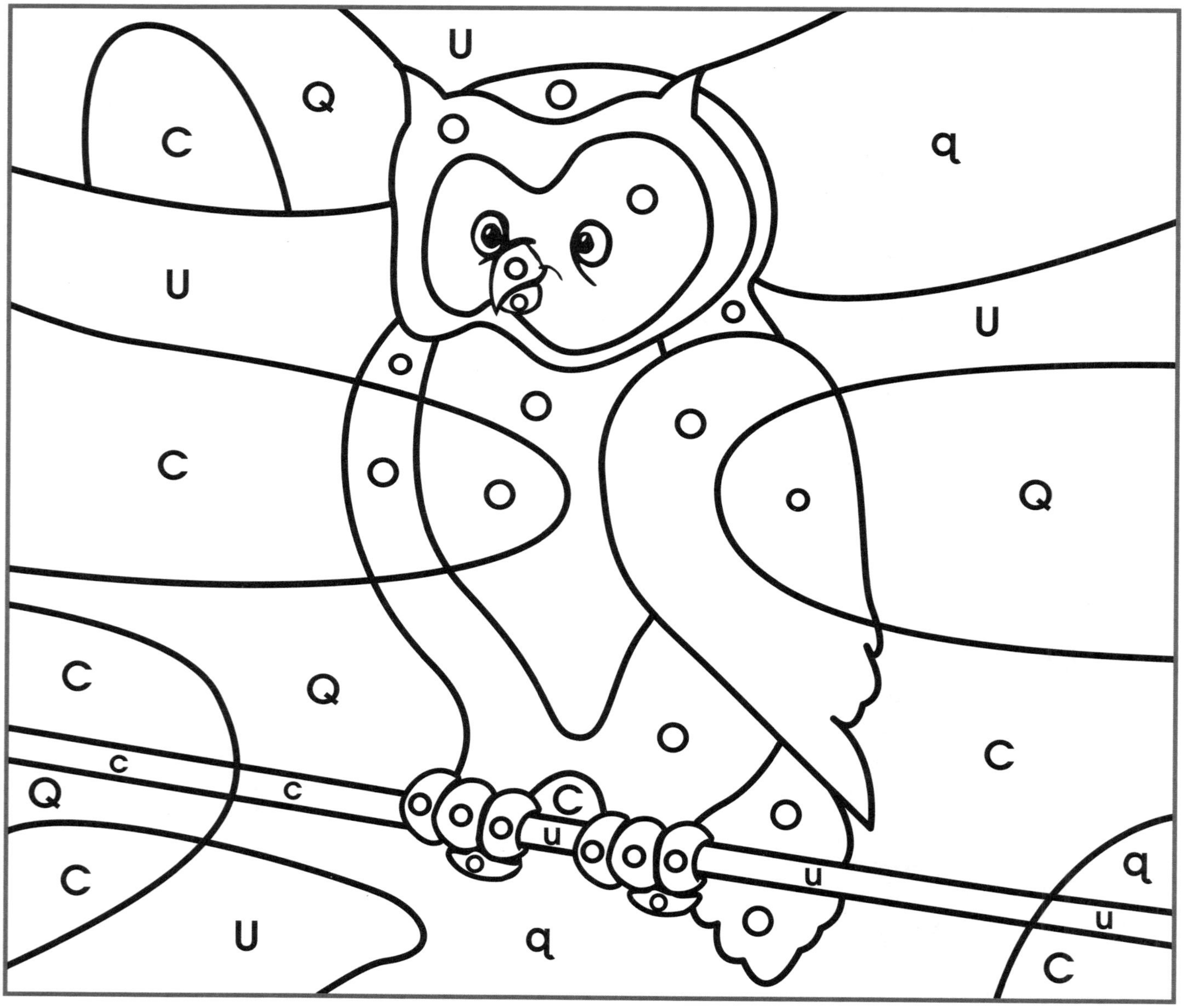

NAME ____________________

Lesson 3 The Letters **O**, **C**, **U**, **S**

Say the letter **C**. Trace it. Write it on the line.

C c

Say each word. Write the missing letter **c** on the line.

___up

___ow

___ap

___ast

___at

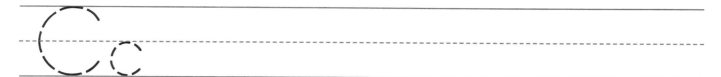

___ut

NAME ____________________

Lesson 3 The Letters **O, C, U, S**

Say the letter **U**. Trace it. Write it on the line.

U u

Follow the letters **U** and **u** to help the girl find her umbrella.

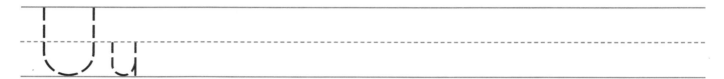

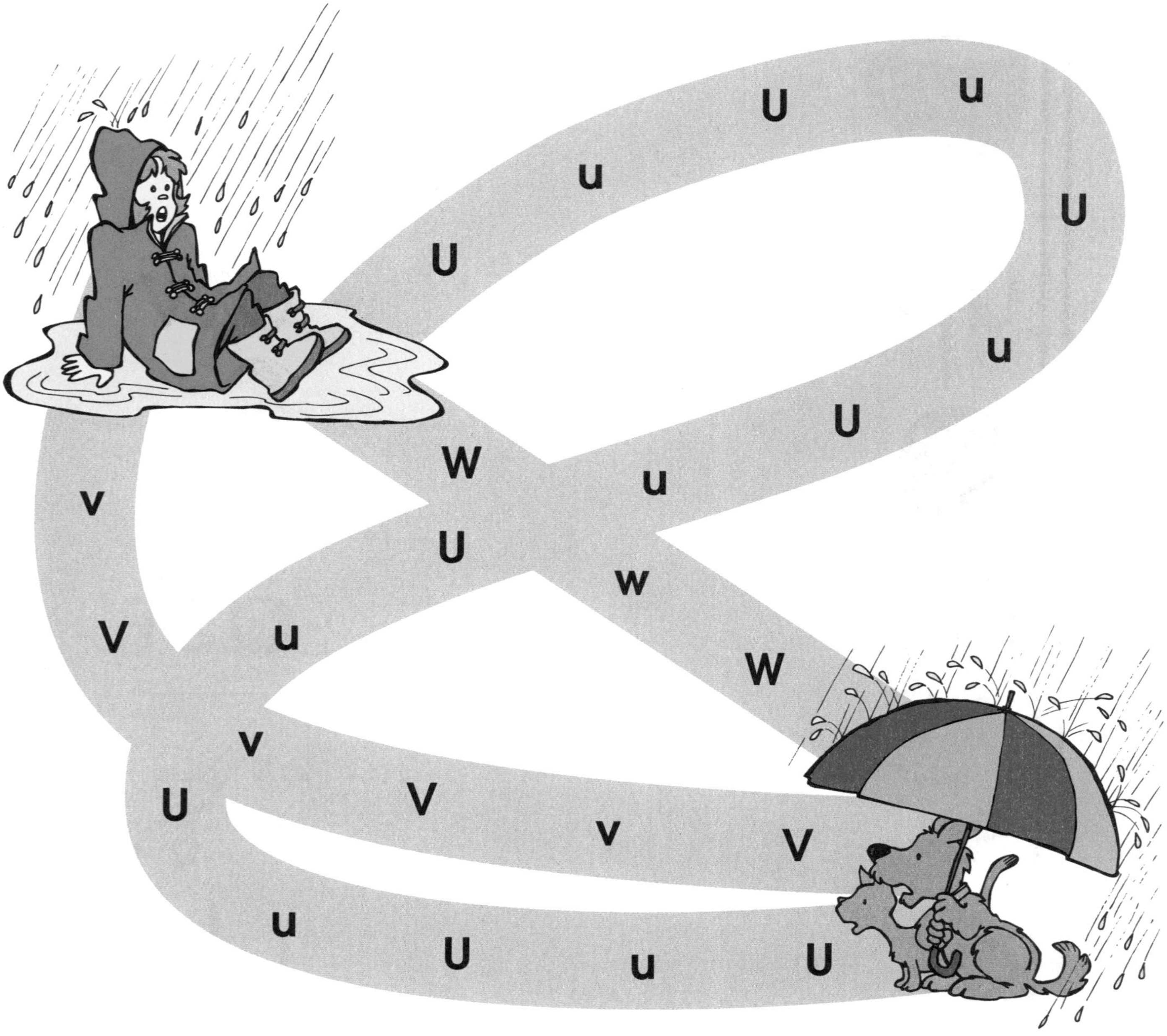

NAME ______________________________

Lesson 3 The Letters **O, C, U, S**

Say the letter **S**. Trace it. Write it on the line.

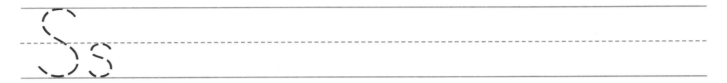

Circle the letter **s** in each word.

NAME ______________________________

Review Lessons 1–3

Say each picture name. Draw a line between the pictures that start with the same letter.

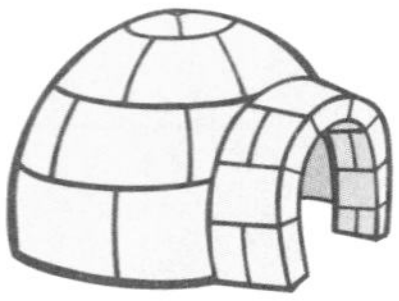
igloo

lamp

kite

vase

yak

sun

van

yo-yo

ice cream

snake

key

log

NAME ____________________

Review Lessons 1–3

Say each picture name. Circle the letter that it begins with. Write the letter on the line.

h z

w v

a o

t h

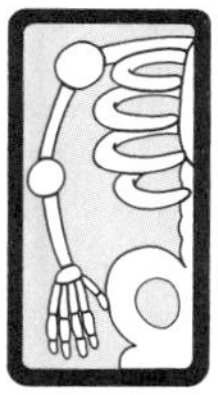

x w

m u

d c

Lesson 4 The Letters **J**, **G**, **P**, **B**

Say the letter **J**. Trace it. Write it on the line.

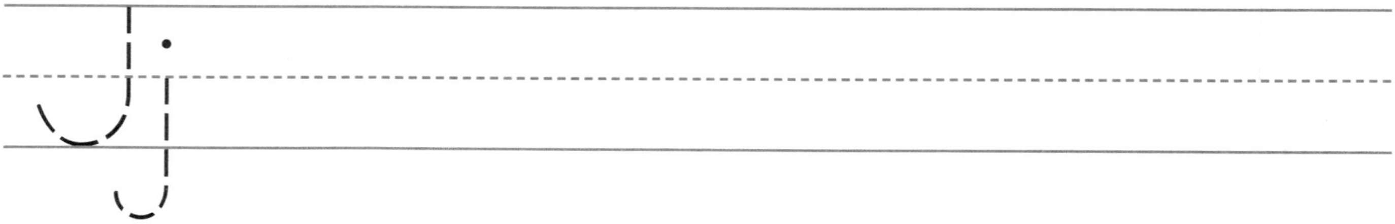

Color the jam jars with a capital **J** red. Color the jam jars with a lowercase **j** purple.

NAME ______________________

Lesson 4 The Letters **J**, **G**, **P**, **B**

Say the letter **G**. Trace it. Write it on the line.

Gg

Say each word. Write the missing letter **g** on the line.

___rass

___oat

___irl

___um

___as

___ate

NAME ____________________

Lesson 4 The Letters **J**, **G**, **P**, **B**

Say the letter **P**. Trace it. Write it on the line.

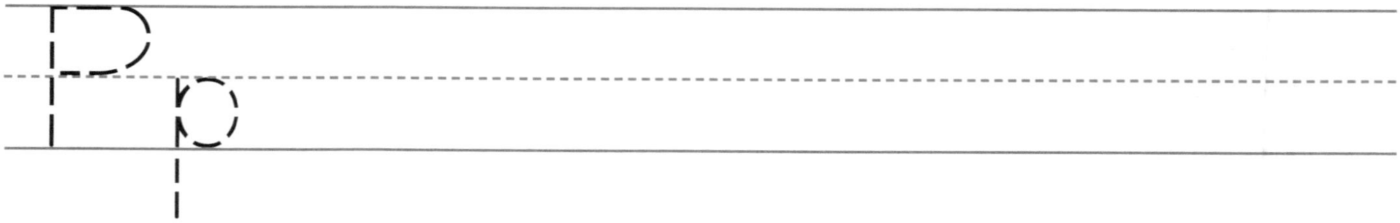

Follow the letters **P** and **p** to help the pig get back to the barn.

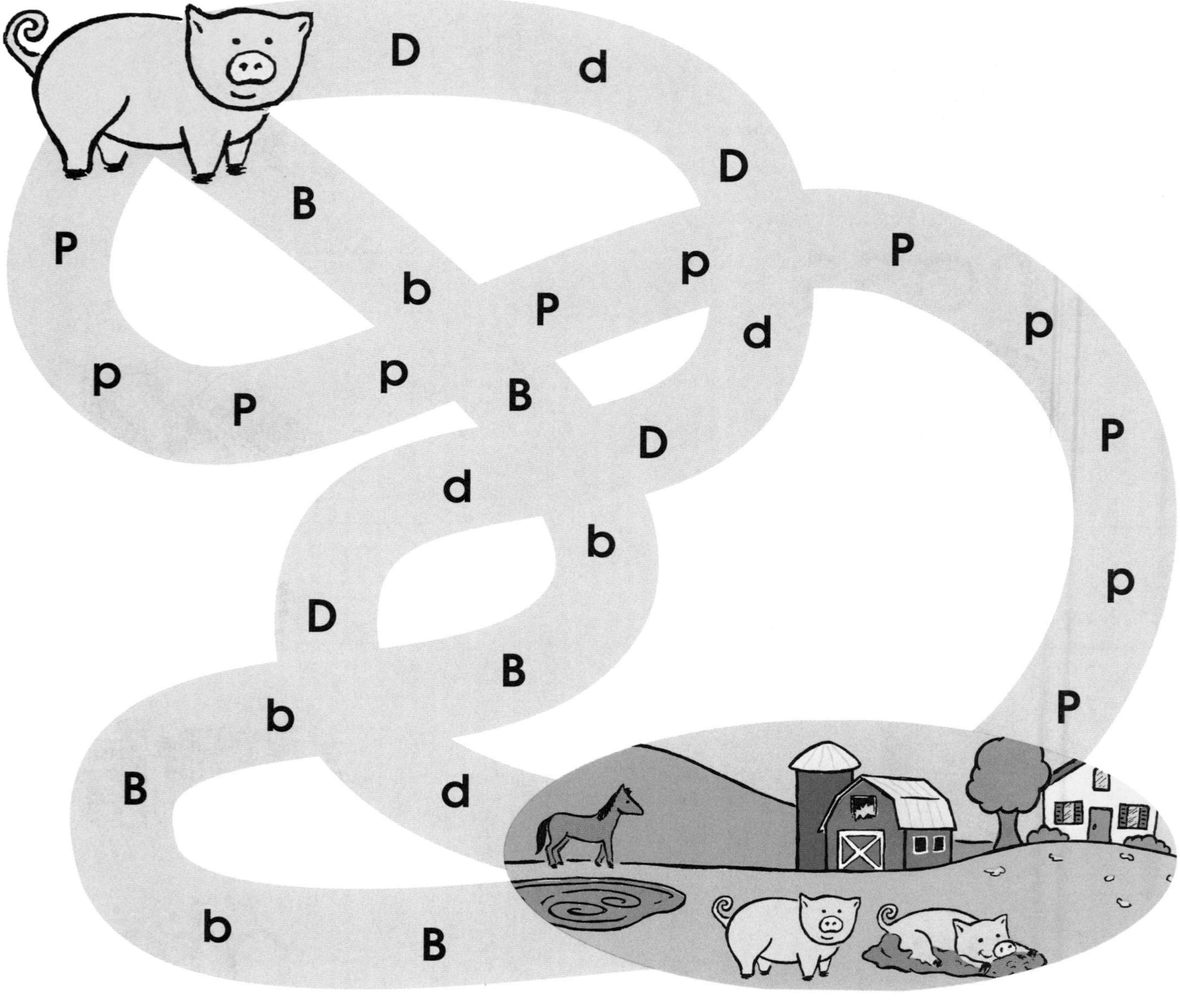

NAME ____________________

Lesson 4 The Letters **J**, **G**, **P**, **B**

Say the letter **B**. Trace it. Write it on the line.

B b

Circle the letter **b** in each word.

bus

boots

bell

book

bat

bug

NAME ______________________

Lesson 5 The Letters **D**, **H**, **M**, **N**, **A**

Say the letter **D**. Trace it. Write it on the line.

Dd

Say the letter **H**. Trace it. Write it on the line.

Hh

Find the hidden picture. Color the spaces with **Dd** or **Hh**.

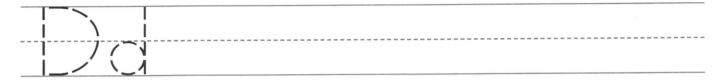

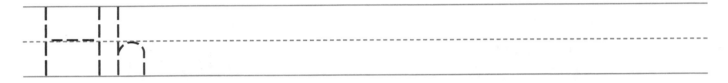

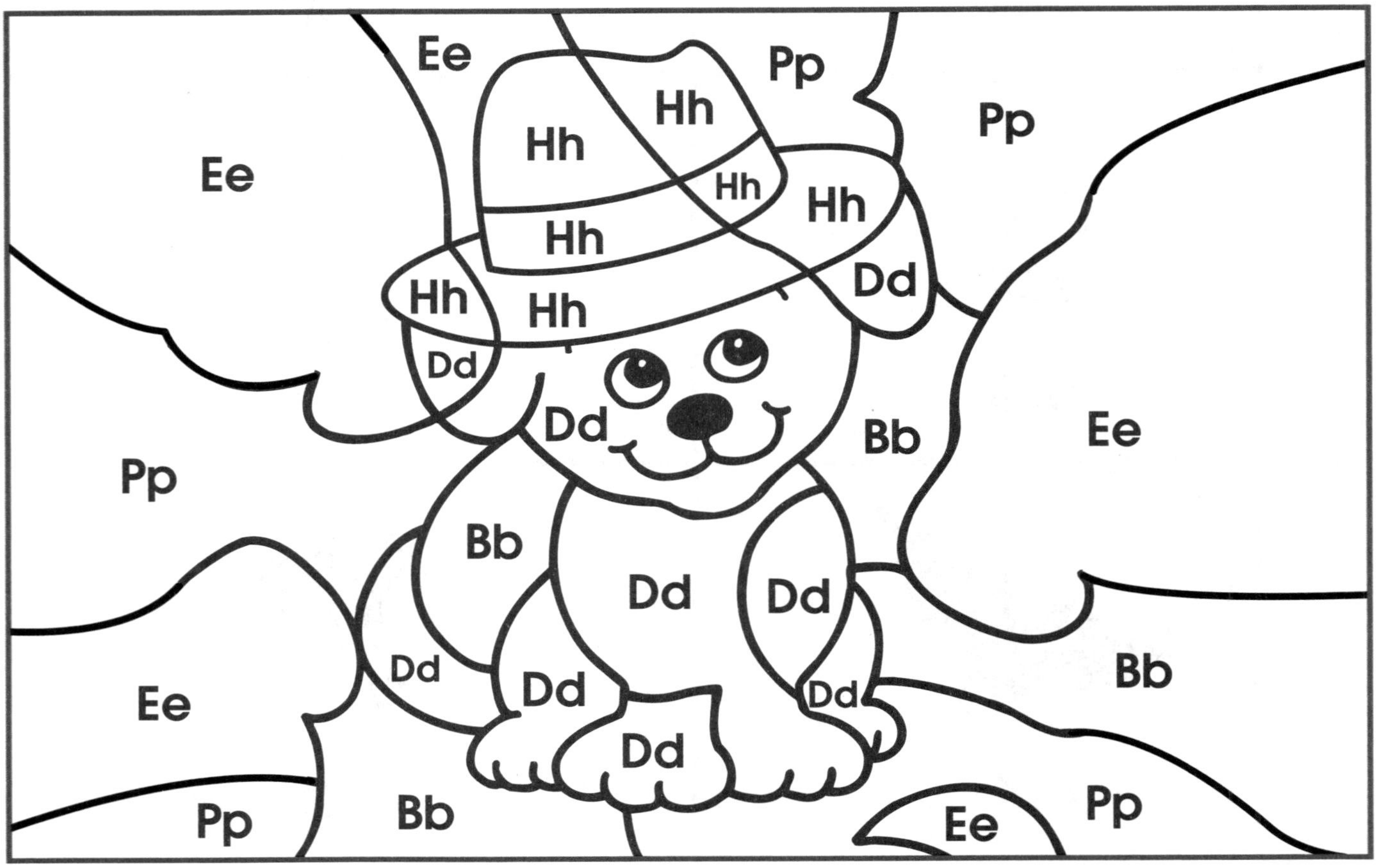

NAME ______________________

Lesson 5 The Letters **D**, **H**, **M**, **N**, **A**

Say the letter **M**. Trace it. Write it on the line.

Mm

Say each word. Write the missing letter **m** on the line.

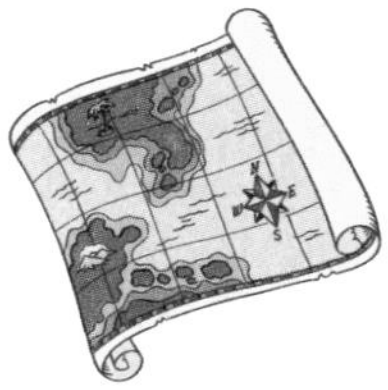

__ap

__oon

__ouse

__op

__ilk

__an

Lesson 5 The Letters **D**, **H**, **M**, **N**, **A**

Say the letter **N**. Trace it. Write it on the line.

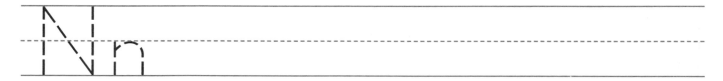

Find the hidden picture. Color the spaces with **N** or **n**.

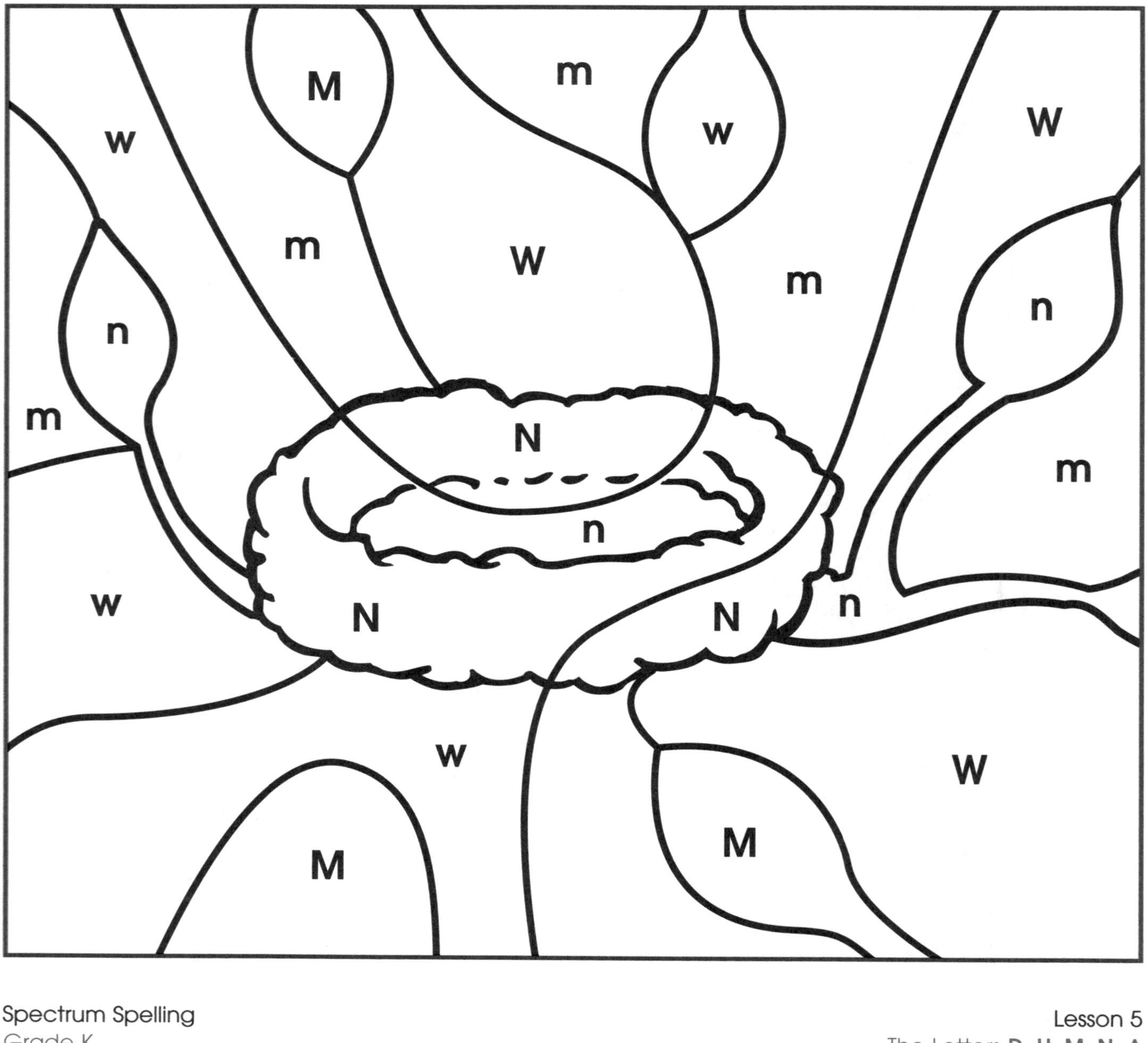

NAME ____________________

Lesson 5 The Letters **D, H, M, N, A**

Say the letter **A**. Trace it. Write it on the line.

Aa

Color the apples with a capital **A** red. Color the apples with a lowercase **a** green.

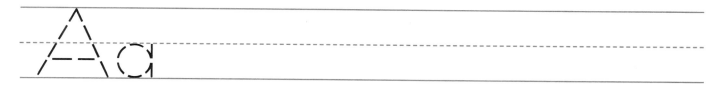

NAME ______________________

Lesson 6 The Letters **E**, **Q**, **R**, **F**

Say the letter **E**. Trace it. Write it on the line.

Circle the letter **e** in each word.

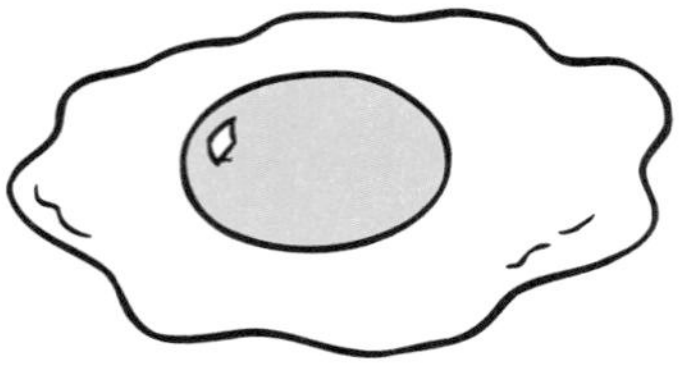

egg

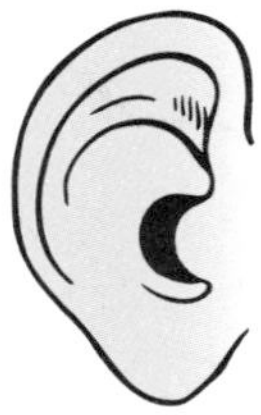

ear

hen

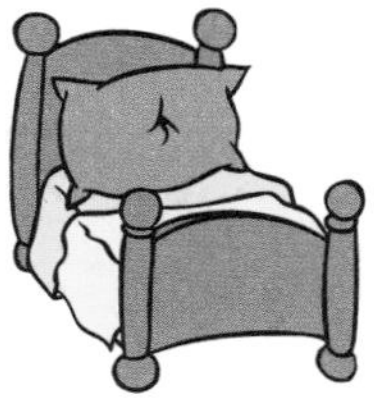

bed

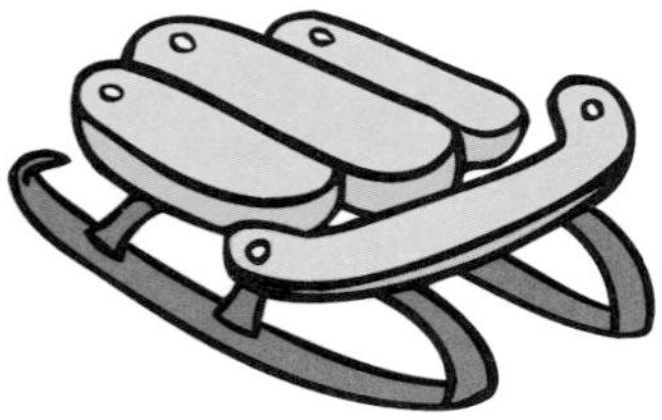

sled

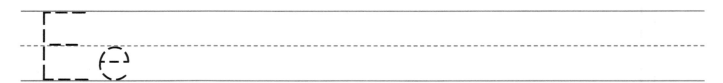

eat

Lesson 6 The Letters **E**, **Q**, **R**, **F**

Say the letter **Q**. Trace it. Write it on the line.

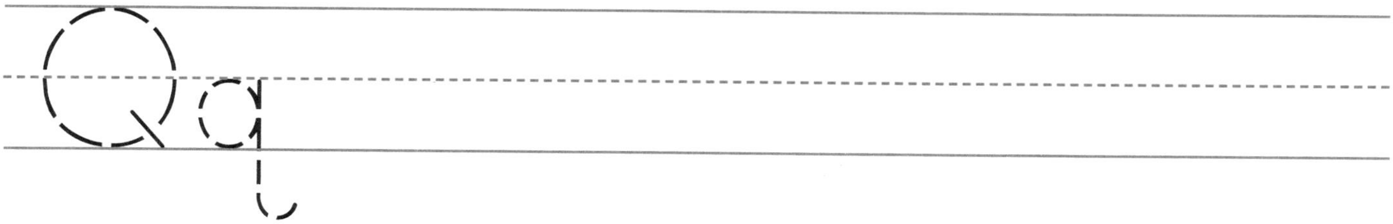

Follow the letters **Q** and **q** to help the queen find her quilt.

Lesson 6 The Letters **E, Q, R, F**

Say the letter **R**. Trace it. Write it on the line.

Rr

Say each word. Write the missing letter **r** on the line.

___ing

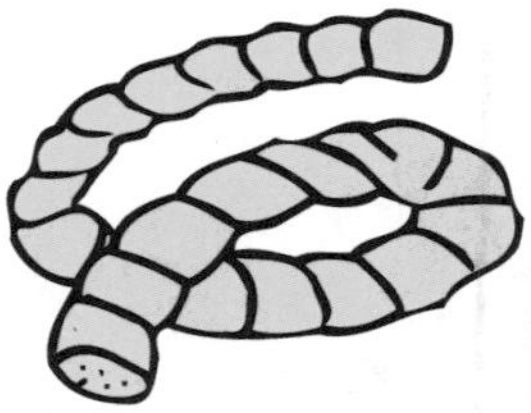

___ope

___ose

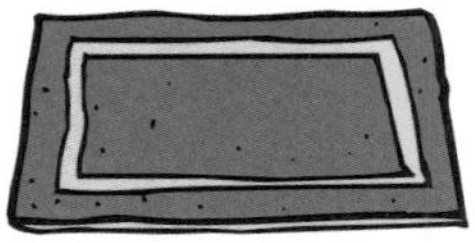

___ug

___ake

___at

NAME ______________________

Lesson 6 The Letters **E, Q, R, F**

Say the letter **F**. Trace it. Write it on the line.

F f

Circle the letter **f** in each word.

fish

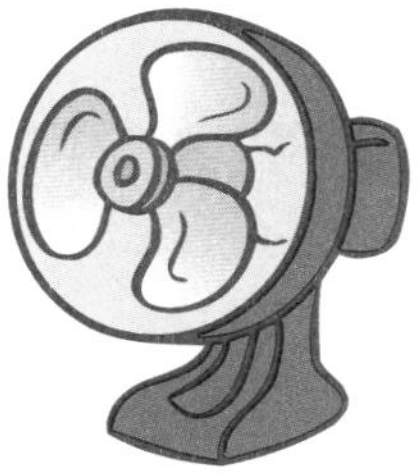

fan

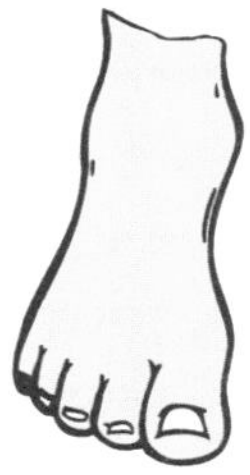

foot

frog

fly

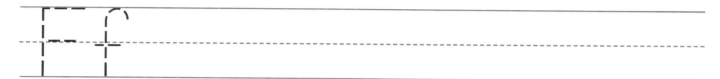

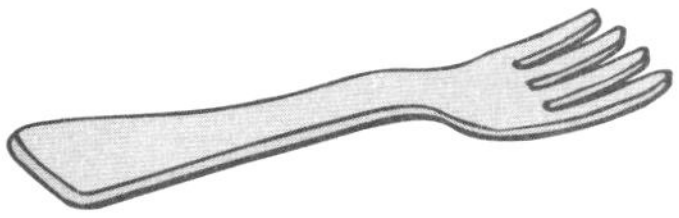

fork

NAME ______________________

Review Lessons 4–6

Say each picture name. Write the missing letter on the line.

quee___

___ox

___nt

___oat

___og

cra___

___ouse

___en

NAME ______________________________

Review Lessons 4–6

Say each picture name. Draw a line between the pictures that start with the same letter.

jam

piano

house

net

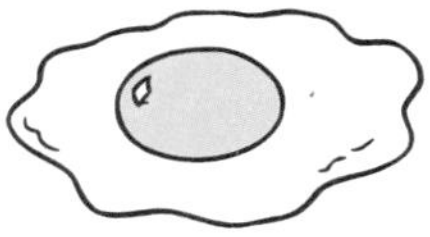
egg

rake

elephant

red

pan

jar

nine

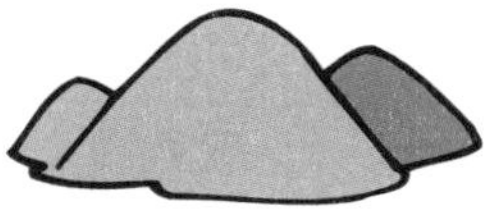
hill

NAME ____________________

Lesson 7 Beginning Sounds /t/, /m/, /s/

Circle the words in each row that start with /m/, like **mouse**.

mat **nose** **milk** **bike**

Circle the words in each row that start with /t/, like **tiger**.

pot **hug** **top** **tent**

Circle the words in each row that start with /s/, like **sun**.

sad **zebra** **car** **soap**

NAME ____________________

Lesson 7 Beginning Sounds /t/, /m/, /s/

Say the name of each picture. Match the pictures that start with the same sound.

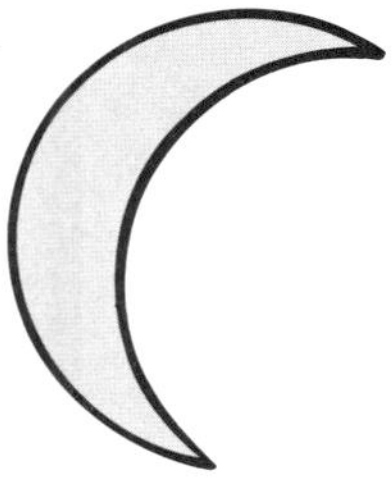

moon

nest

map

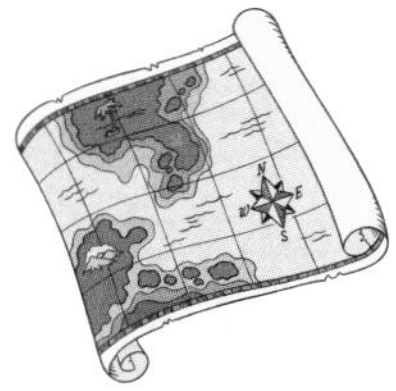

top

tent

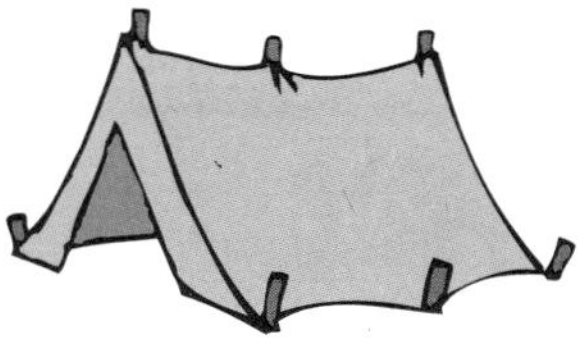

sock

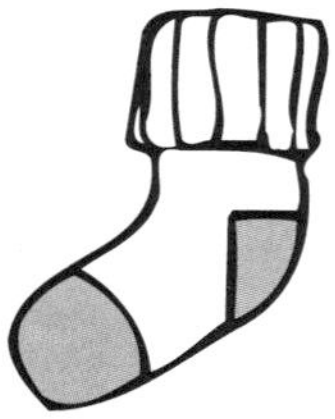

soap

candle

sand

NAME ___________________

Lesson 8 Beginning Sounds /j/, /k/, /d/, /f/

Say the name of each picture. Fill in the missing letter for each word.

___eather

___am

___og

___at

___an

NAME ____________________

Lesson 8 Beginning Sounds /j/, /k/, /d/, /f/

Circle the pictures in each row with the same beginning sound. Write the letter for the sound.

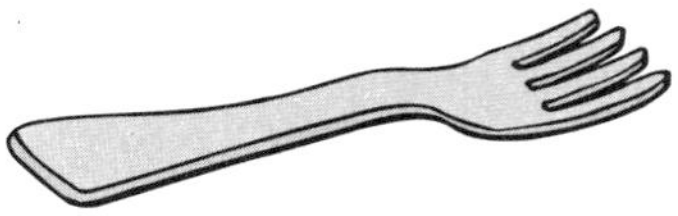

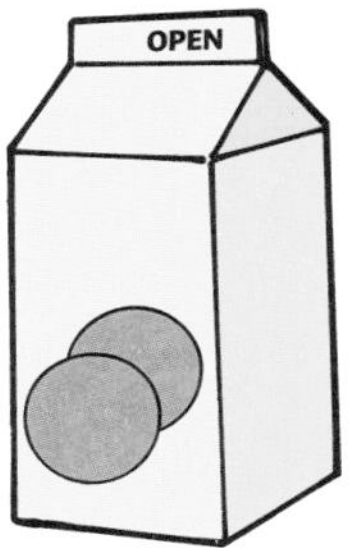

NAME ____________________

Review Lessons 7–8

Circle the words in each row that start with /k/, like **kite**.
Write the letter **k** on the line.

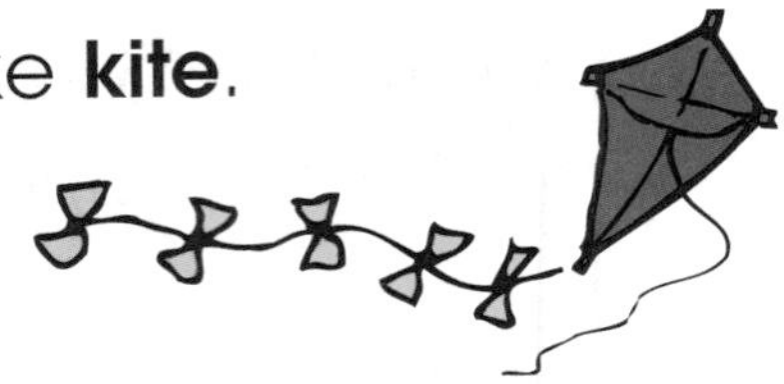

king **hit** **ten** **key** ________

Circle the words in each row that start with /d/, like **dog**.
Write the letter **d** on the line.

bed **dam** **can** **doll** ________

Circle the words in each row that start with /t/, like **turtle**.
Write the letter **t** on the line.

juice **hug** **top** **train** ________

LESSONS 7–8 REVIEW

NAME ____________________

Review Lessons 7–8

Say each picture name. Circle the letter for the beginning sound. Write the letter on the line.

t h ______

t f ______

s c ______

w m ______

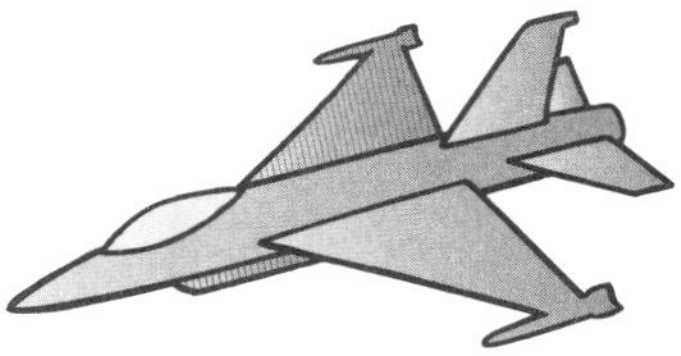

y j ______

NAME ________________________________

Lesson 9 Beginning Sounds /g/, /n/, /w/

Circle the words in each row that start with /w/, like **worm**.

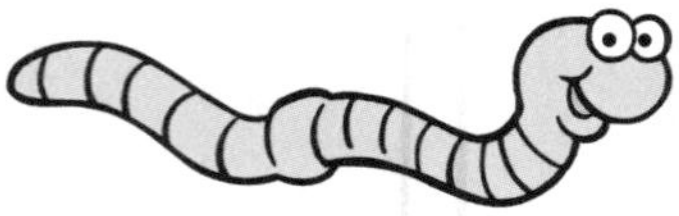

window **mask** **web** **violin**

Circle the words in each row that start with /n/, like **nine**.

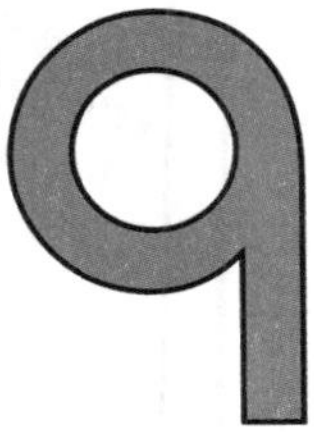

mine **nice** **us** **net**

Circle the words in each row that start with /g/, like **gate**.

queen **gum** **game** **yes**

NAME ______________________

Lesson 9 Beginning Sounds /g/, /n/, /w/

Color the pictures in each row with the same beginning sound. Write the letter for the sound.

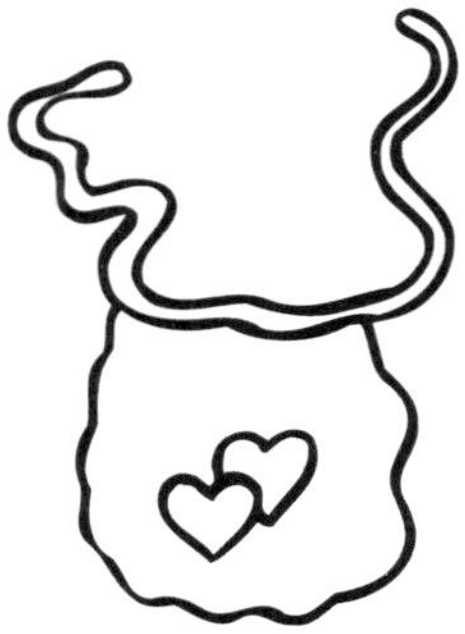

NAME ______________________

Lesson 10 Beginning Sounds /b/, /h/, /p/

Say the name of each picture. Fill in the missing letter for each word.

___ug

___at

___umpkin

___oy

___ail

NAME ________________________________

Lesson 10 Beginning Sounds /b/, /h/, /p/

Say the name of each picture. Match the pictures that start with the same sound.

bus

hill

bird

hammer

box

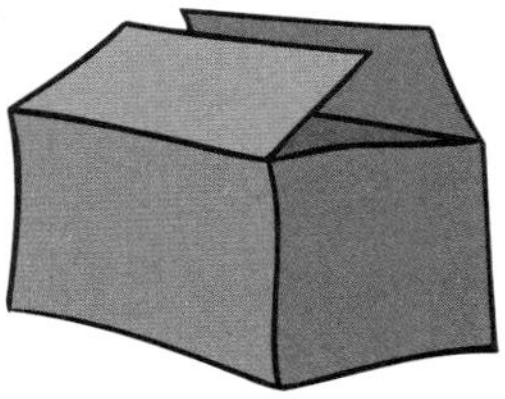

hand

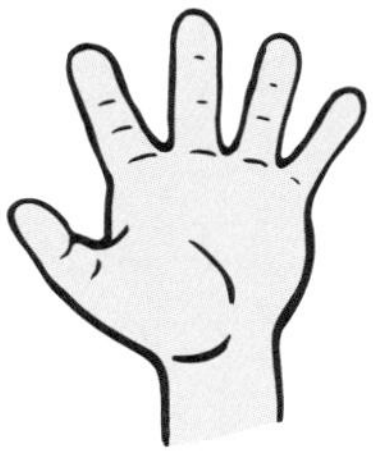

piano

penguin

kite

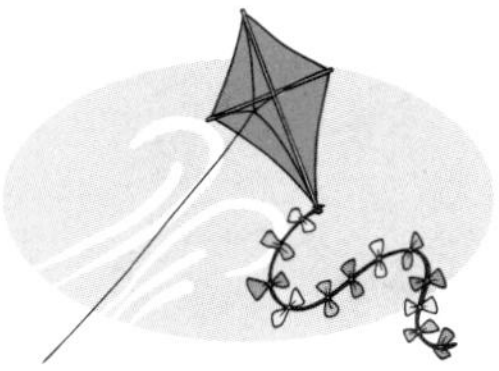

NAME ____________________

Review Lessons 9–10

Color each picture that starts with the /w/ sound.

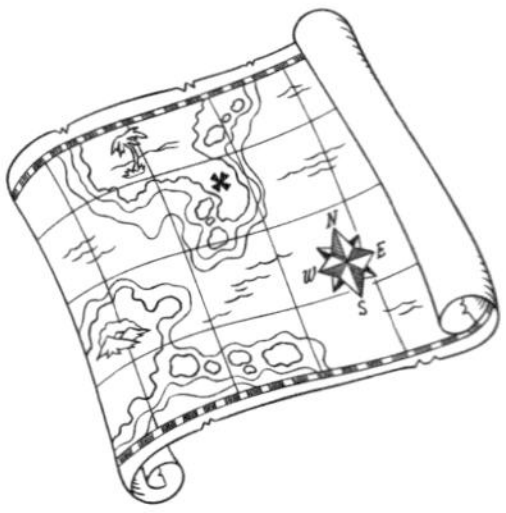

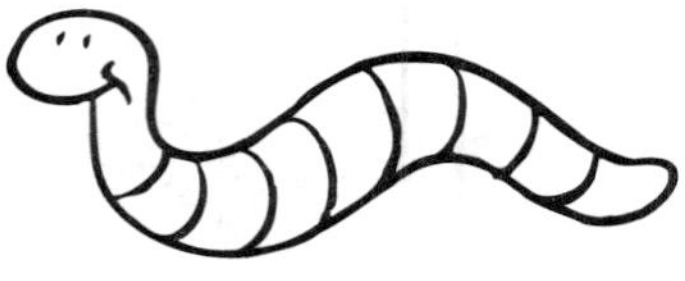

Color each picture that starts with the /p/ sound.

Color each picture that starts with the /b/ sound.

Color each picture that starts with the /g/ sound.

NAME ______________________________

Review Lessons 9–10

Say the name of each picture. Fill in the missing letter for each word.

___ose

___at

___ot

___eb

___oose

NAME ______________________

Lesson 11 Beginning Sounds /r/, /k/, /l/

Circle the pictures in each row with the same beginning sound. Write the letter for the sound.

   ______

 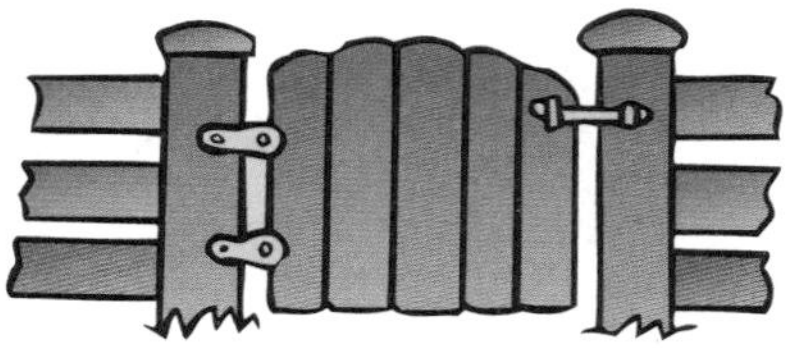  ______

  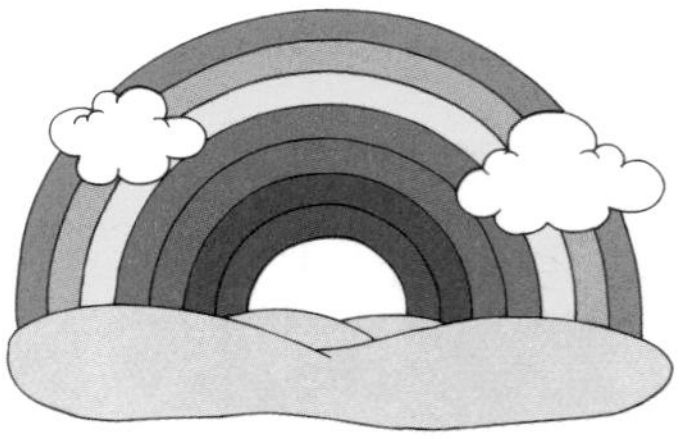 ______

NAME ______________________

Lesson 11 Beginning Sounds /r/, /k/, /l/

Say the name of each picture. Fill in the missing letter for each word.

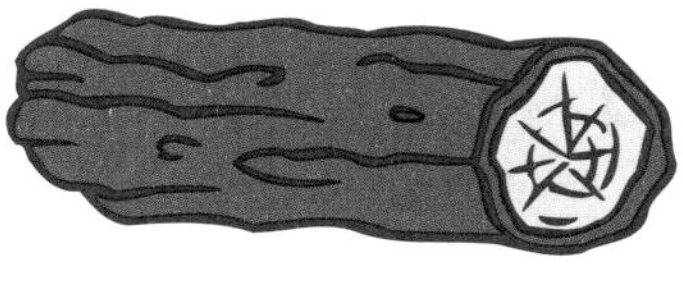

___og

___ite

___ing

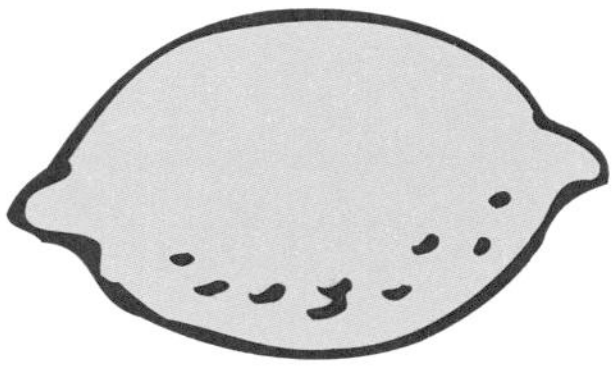

___emon

___ug

NAME ______________________________

Lesson 12 Beginning Sounds /v/, /y/, /z/

Say the name of each picture. Match the pictures that start with the same sound.

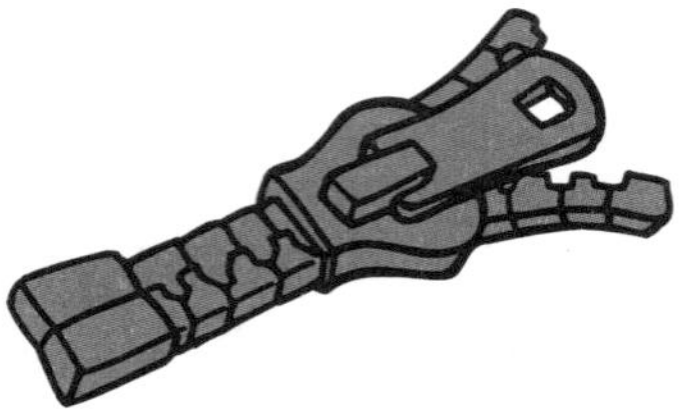

zipper

zebra

sled

vase

watch

violin

yarn

wig

yo-yo

NAME ____________________

Lesson 12 Beginning Sounds /v/, /y/, /z/

Circle the words in each row that start with /z/, like **zoo**.

fun **zebra** **sat** **zip**

Circle the words in each row that start with /v/, like **van**.

vet **up** **worm** **vase**

Circle the words in each row that start with /y/, like **yo-yo**.

yellow **wet** **yak** **yes**

NAME ______________________

Review Lessons 11–12

Say the name of each picture. Match the pictures that start with the same sound.

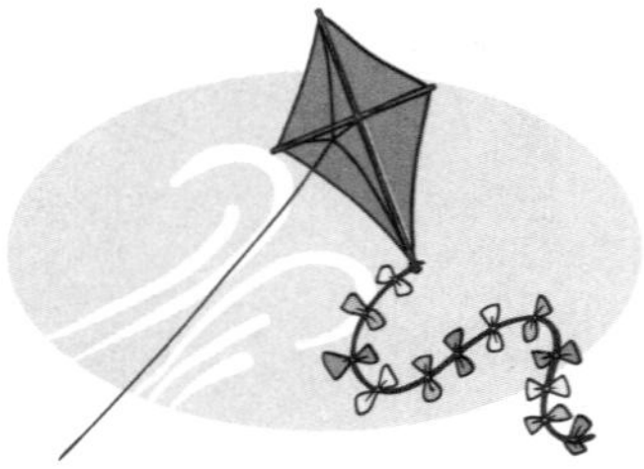

kite

king

house

ring

penguin

rope

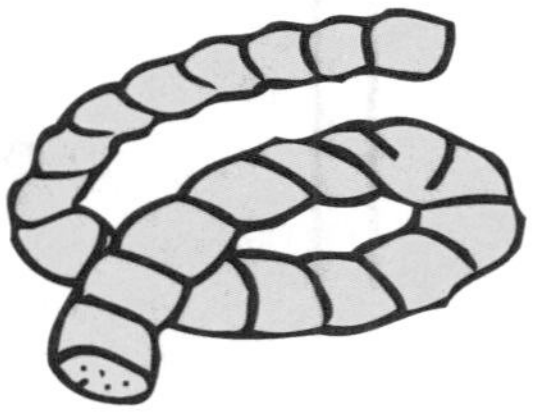

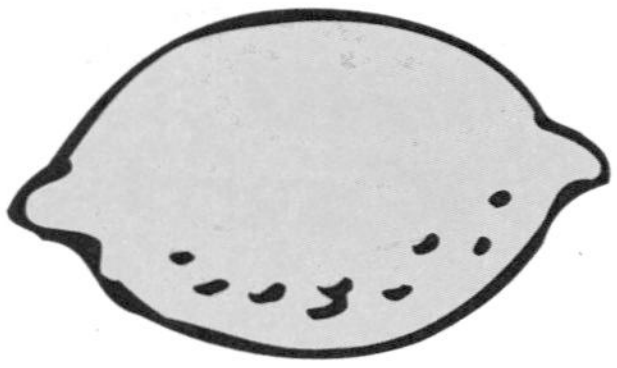

lemon

tent

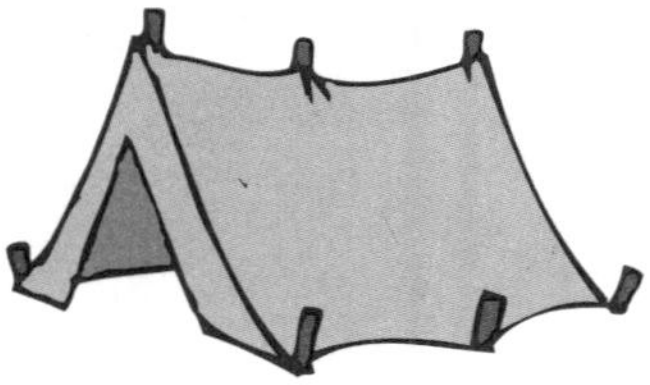

leaf

NAME ______________________

Review Lessons 11–12

Say each picture name. Write the letter for the beginning sound. Choose from the letters in the box.

r v y z

 ______

 ______

 ______

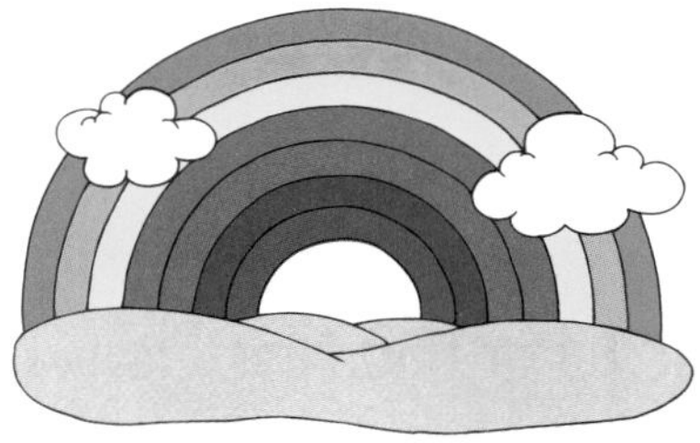 ______

 ______

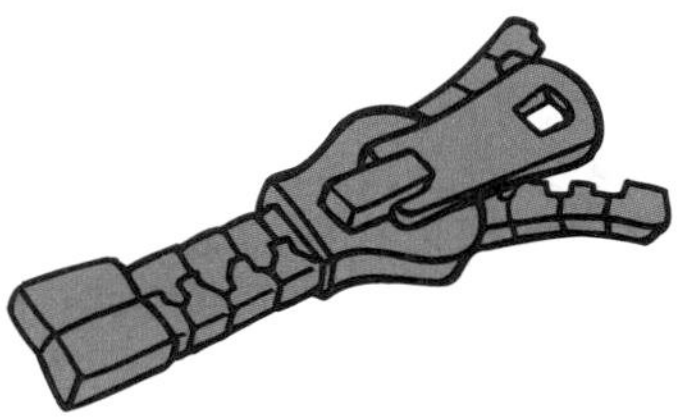 ______

NAME ______________________

Lesson 13 Ending Sounds /d/, /t/, /m/

Color each picture that ends with the /d/ sound.

Color each picture that ends with the /t/ sound.

Color each picture that ends with the /m/ sound.

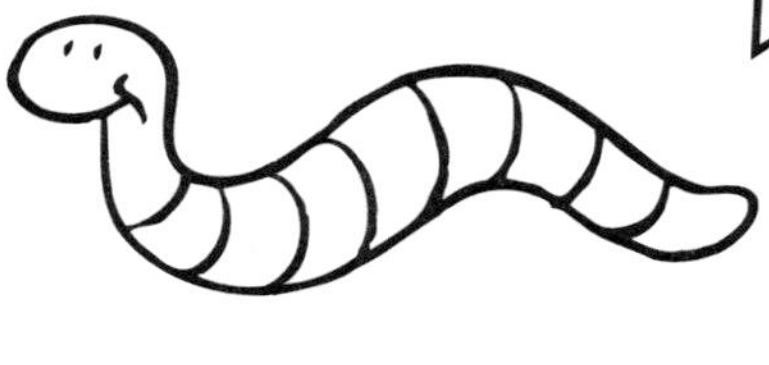

NAME ______________________

Lesson 13 Ending Sounds /d/, /t/, /m/

Say the name of each picture. Fill in the missing letter for each word.

an___

swi___

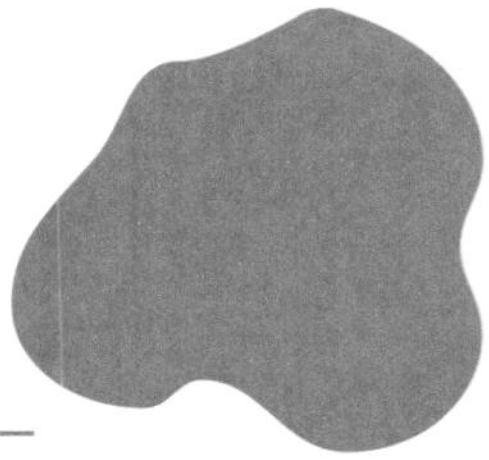

re___

boo___

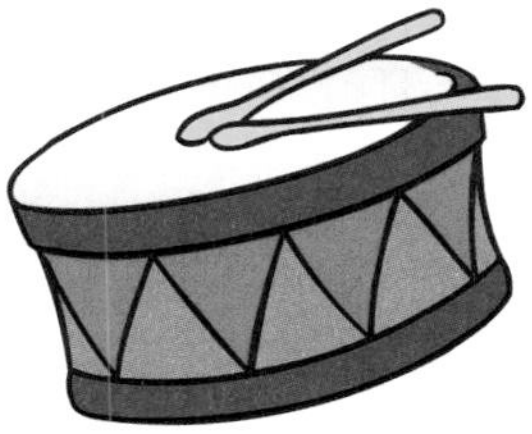

dru___

clou___

NAME ______________________________

Lesson 14 Ending Sounds /s/, /g/, /b/

Circle the words in each row that end with /s/, like **gas**.

sock **ship** **grass** **mess**

Circle the words in each row that end with /g/, like **leg**.

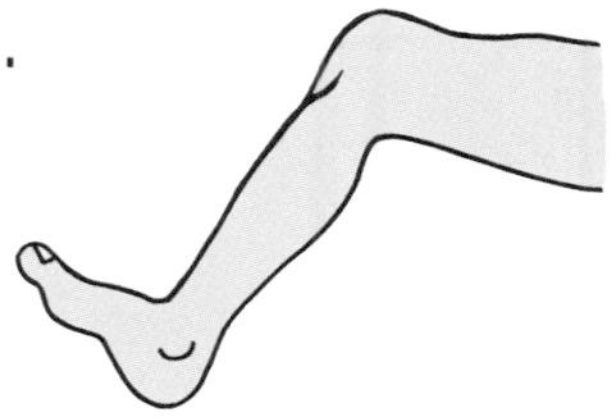

egg **lick** **flag** **play**

Circle the words in each row that end with /b/, like **crab**.

map **tub** **crib** **hat**

NAME ______________________________

Lesson 14 Ending Sounds /s/, /g/, /b/

Circle the pictures in each row with the same ending sound. Write the letter for the sound.

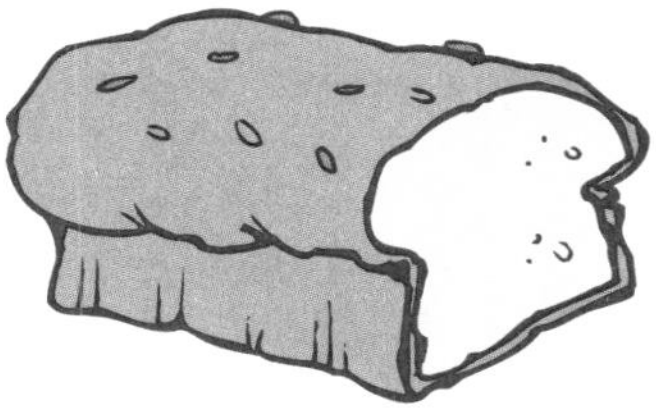

______

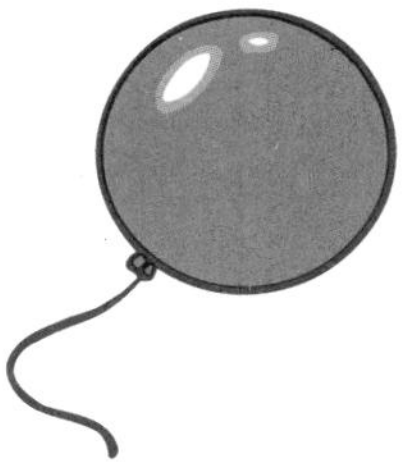

______

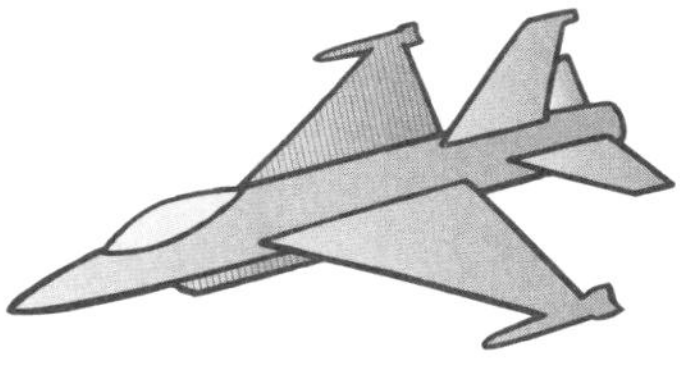
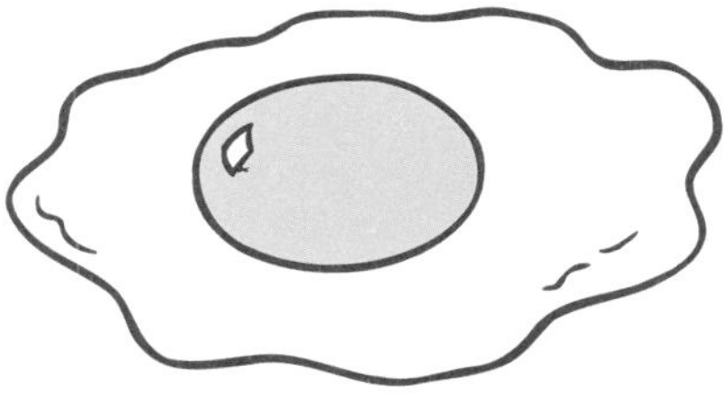

______

NAME ____________________

Lesson 15 Ending Sounds /p/, /n/, /x/

Say the name of each picture. Fill in the missing letter for each word.

cla___

fo___

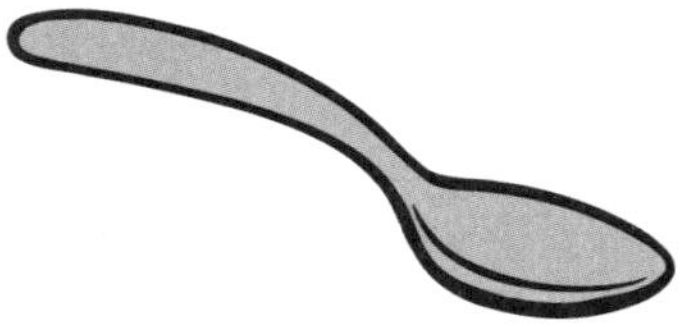

spoo___

sou___

si___

quee___

NAME ______________________

Lesson 15 Ending Sounds /p/, /n/, /x/

Color each picture that ends with the /p/ sound.

Color each picture that ends with the /n/ sound.

Color each picture that ends with the /x/ sound.

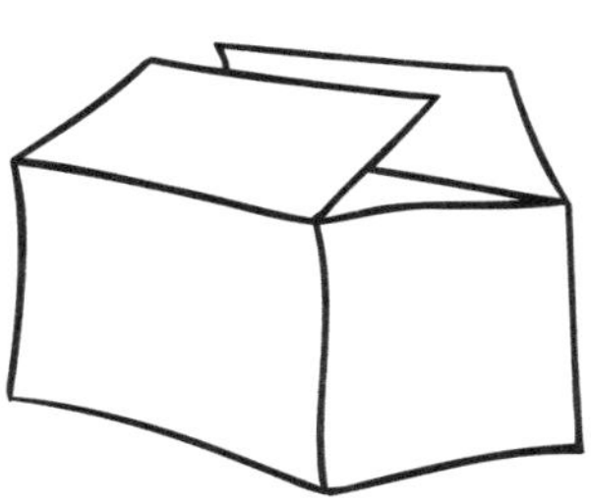

NAME ______________________

Review Lessons 13–15

Say the name of each picture. Match the pictures that end with the same sound.

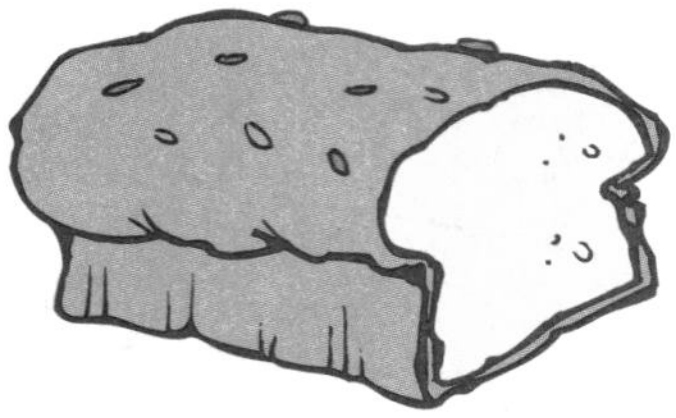

bread

sled

bib

bat

flag

boot

dress

box

grass

NAME ______________________

Review Lessons 13–15

Say the name of each picture. Fill in the missing letter for each word. Choose from the letters in the box.

m x p g b n

cu___

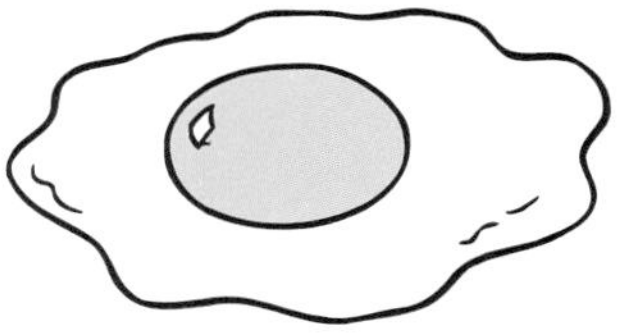

eg___

o___

lio___

tu___

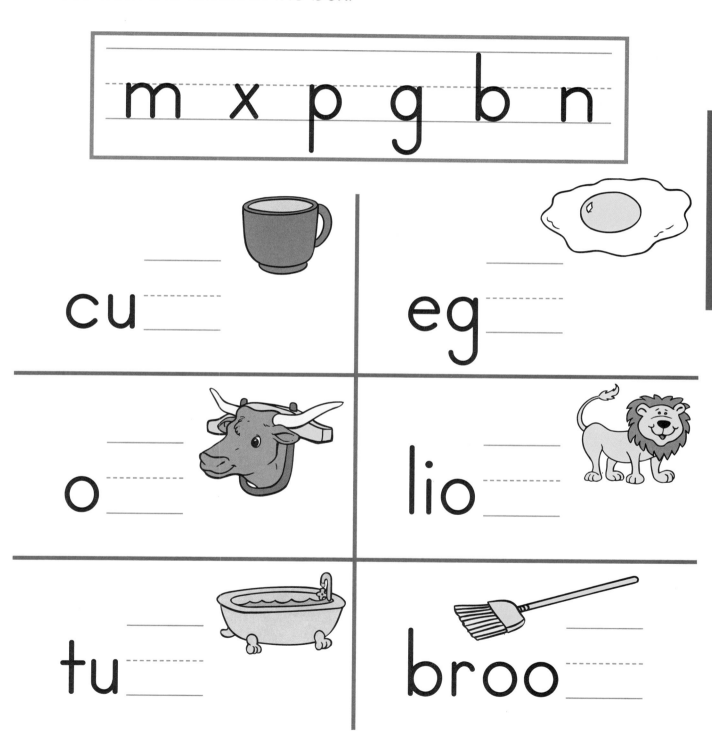

broo___

LESSONS 13–15 REVIEW

Lesson 16 The Short **a** Sound

Help the bat find its cave. Follow the words that have the short **a** sound, like you hear in **pan** .

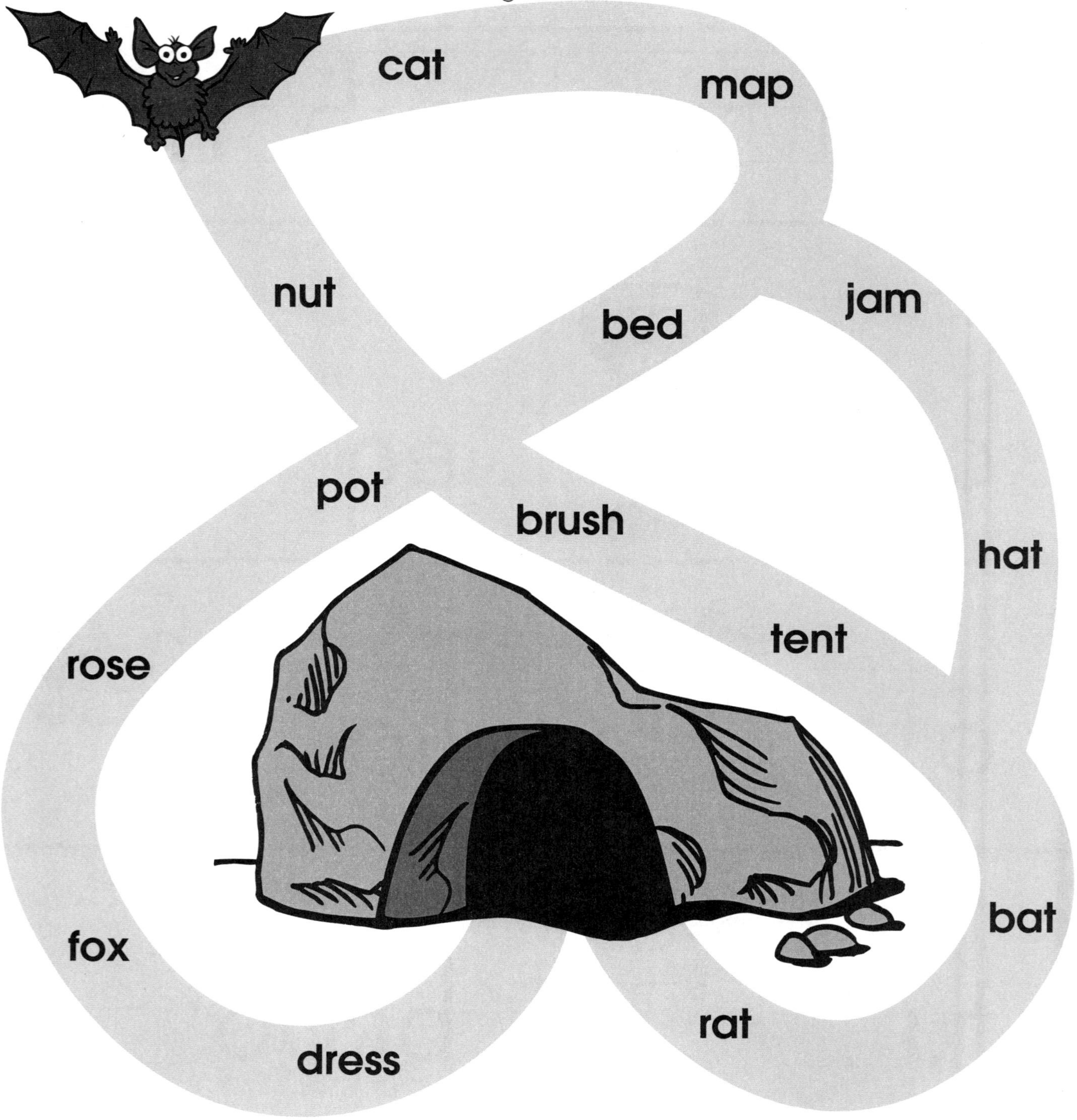

NAME ______________________

Lesson 16 The Short **a** Sound

Say the name of each picture. Fill in the missing letter for each word.

m ___ sk

l ___ mp

c ___ p

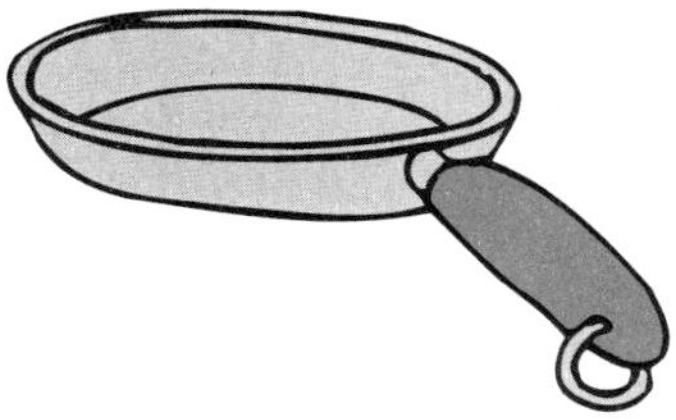

p ___ n

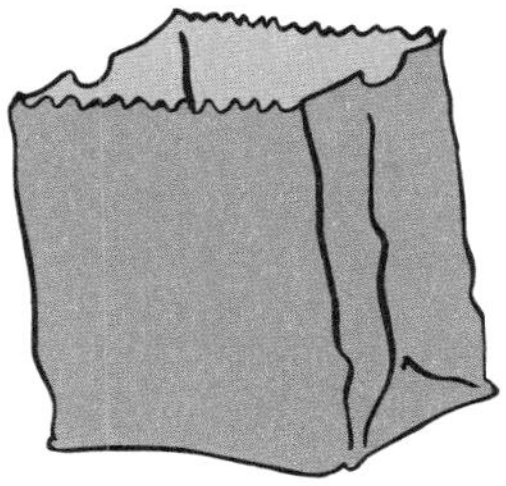

b ___ g

f ___ n

NAME ______________________

Lesson 17 The Short **e** Sound

Say the name of each picture. Circle the pictures that have the short **e** sound, like you hear in **dress**  .

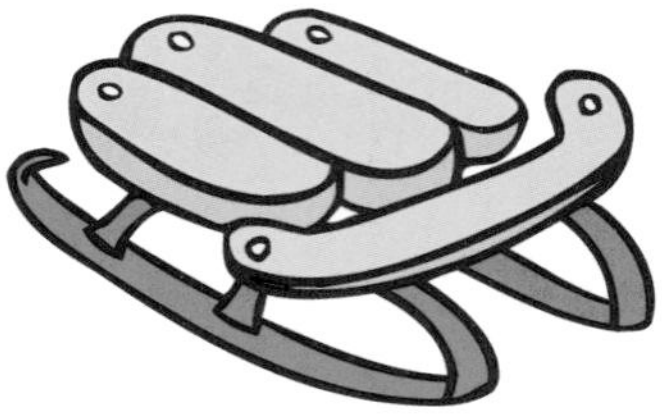

NAME ____________________

Lesson 17 The Short **e** Sound

Draw a line to match the pictures to the words. In each word, circle the short **e** sound, like you hear in **egg** 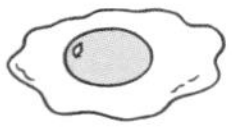 .

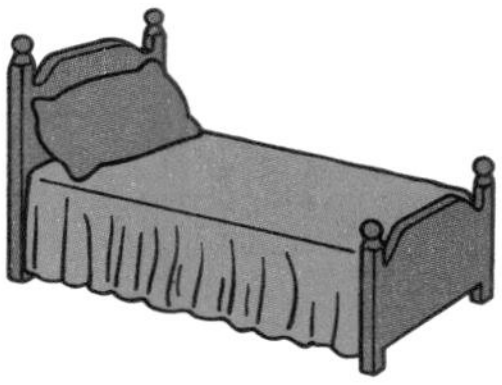

shell

ten

nest

bed

desk

bell

Review Lessons 16–17

Say each picture name. Circle the pictures that have the short **e** sound, like you hear in **ten** 10.

Cross out the pictures that have the short **a** sound, like you hear in **pan** .

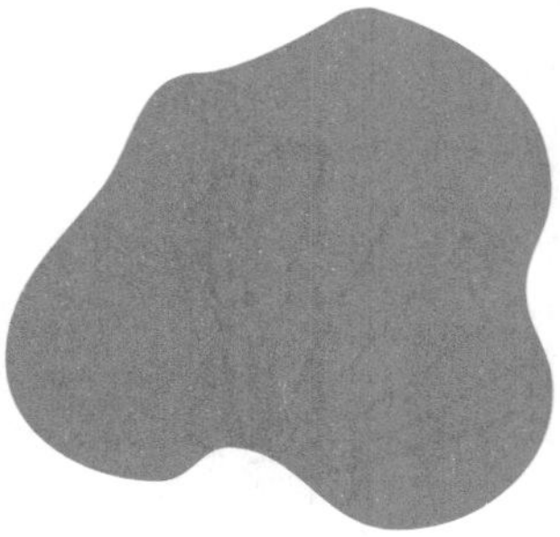

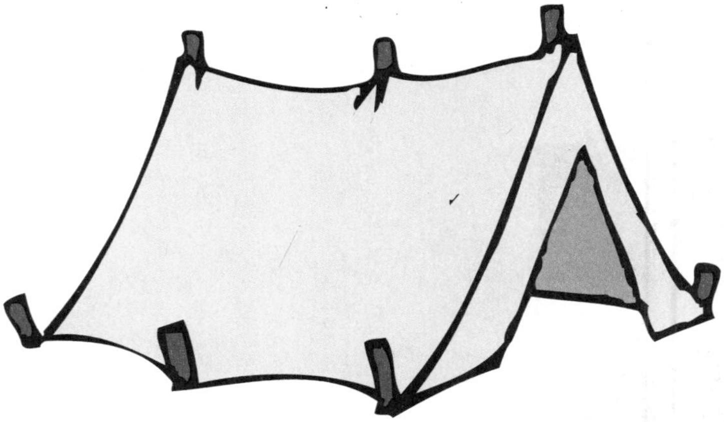

NAME ____________________

Review Lessons 16–17

Say each picture name. Circle the vowel sound you hear in each word. Circle **a** for the sound you hear in **apple**  .

Circle **e** for the sound you hear in **hen**  .

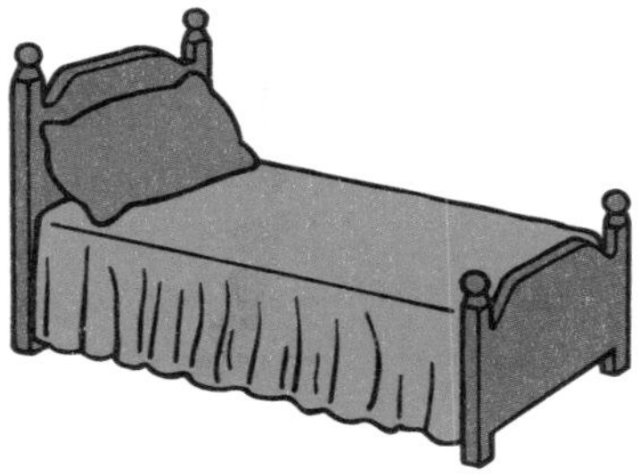

e **a**

e **a**

e **a**

e **a**

e **a**

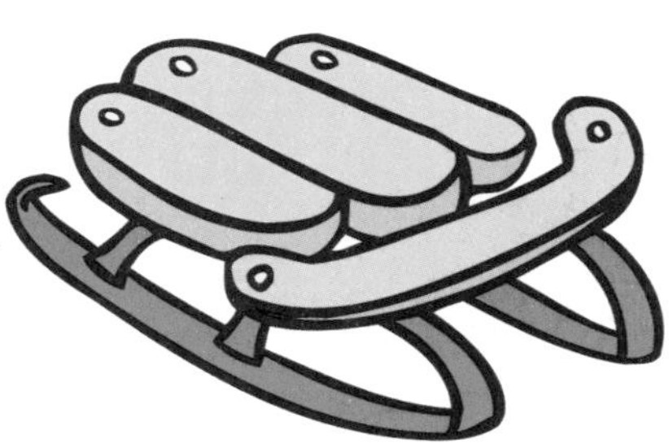

e **a**

NAME ____________________

Lesson 18 The Short **i** Sound

Say the name of each picture. Color the pictures that have the short **i** sound, like you hear in **pink**  .

short i

NAME ____________________

Lesson 18 The Short **i** Sound

Help the girl find her missing mitten. Follow the words with the short **i** sound, like you hear in **fish**  .

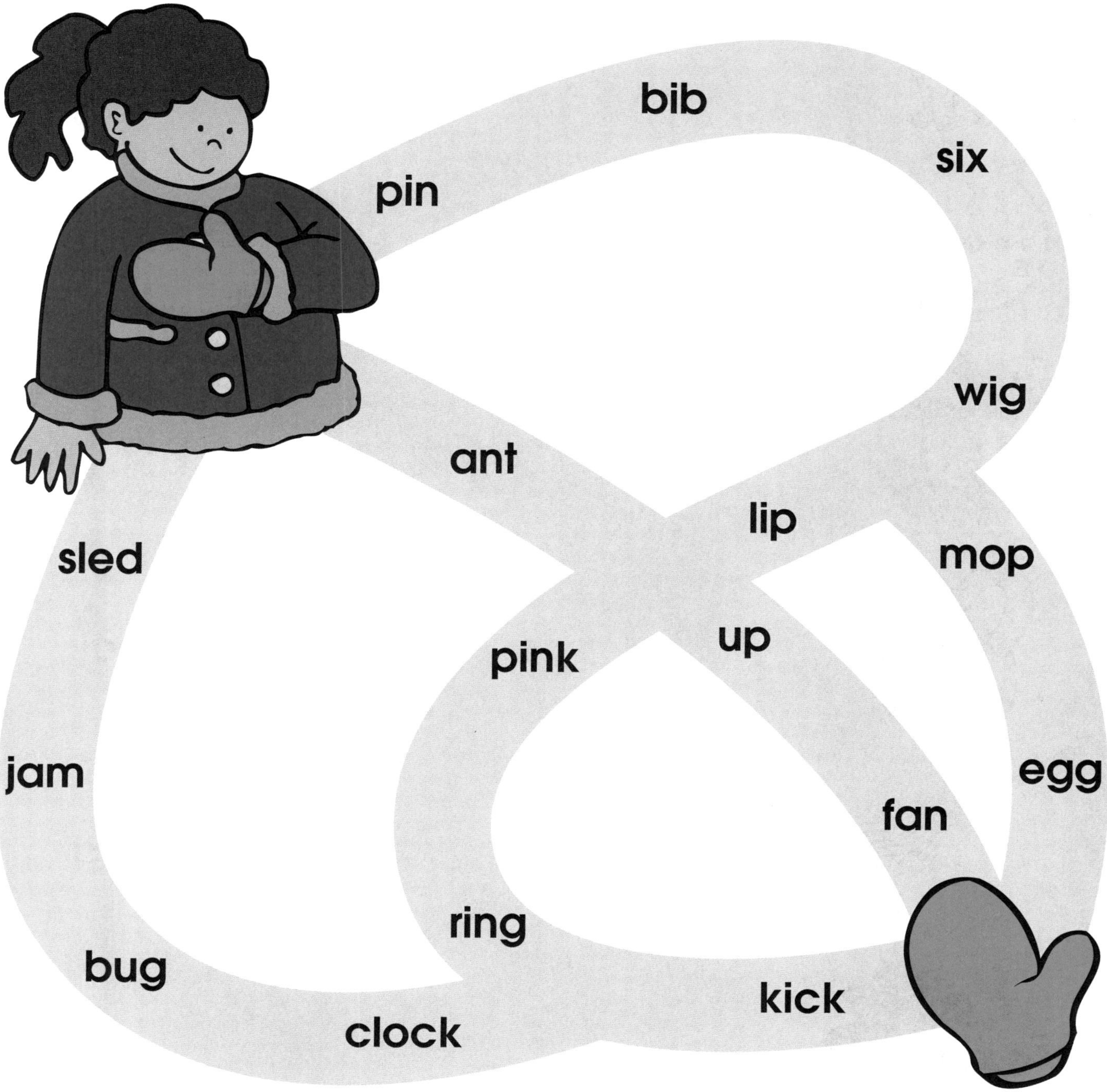

NAME ____________________

Lesson 19 The Short o Sound

Draw a line to match the pictures to the words. In each word, circle the short **o** sound, like you hear in **log**  .

stop

mop

fox

lock

frog

clock

NAME ____________________

Lesson 19 The Short o Sound

Say the name of each picture. Fill in the missing letter for each word.

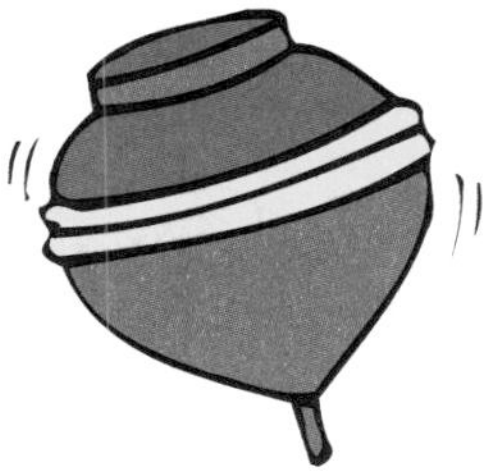

t ___ p

h ___ t

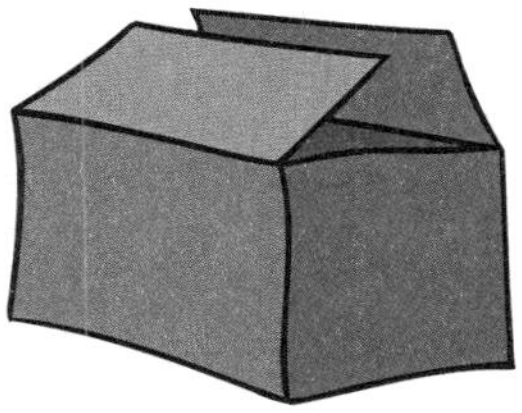

b ___ x

s ___ ck

p ___ p

bl ___ cks

NAME ______________________

Lesson 20 The Short **u** Sound

Say the name of each picture. Circle the pictures in each row that have the short **u** sound, like you hear in **cup**  .

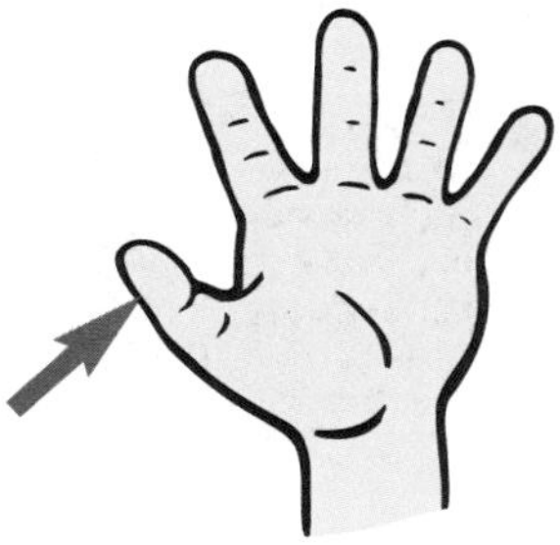

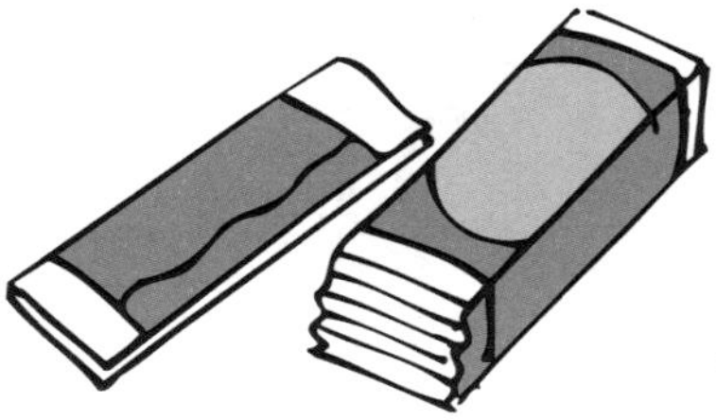

NAME ________________________________

Lesson 20 The Short **u** Sound

Say the name of each picture. Color the pictures that have the short **u** sound, like you hear in **nut**  .

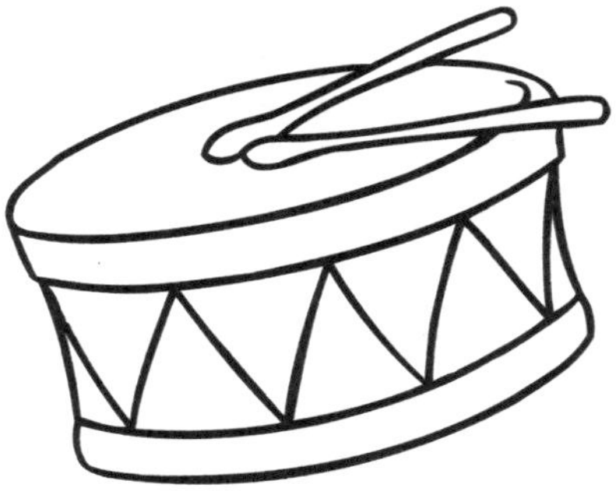

short u

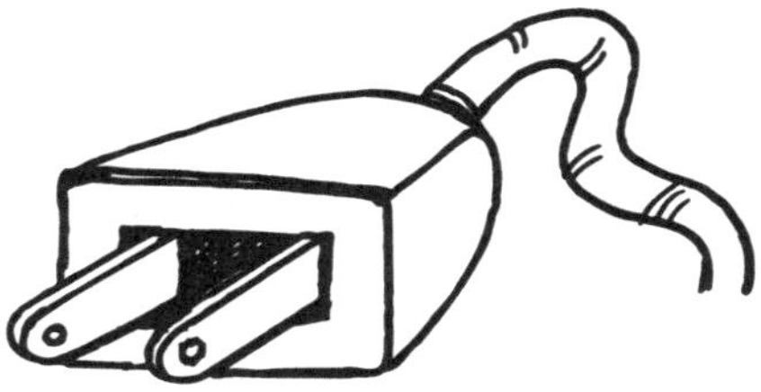

NAME ______________________

Review Lessons 18–20

Say the name of each picture. Circle the pictures in each row that have the short **i** sound, like you hear in **pin**  .

Say the name of each picture. Circle the pictures in each row that have the short **o** sound, like you hear in **lock**  .

 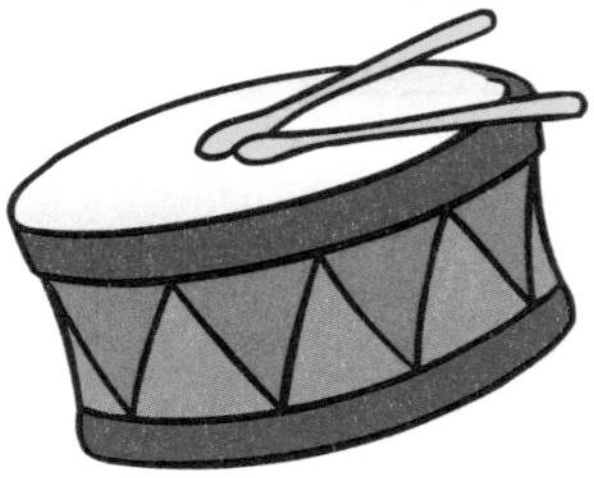  

Say the name of each picture. Circle the pictures in each row that have the short **u** sound, like you hear in **bug**  .

 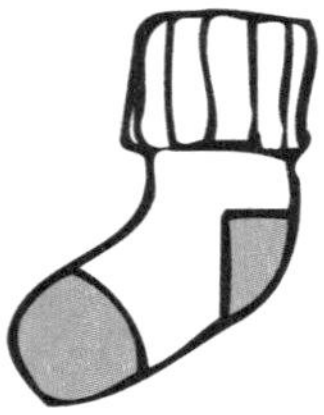  

NAME ___________________

Review Lessons 18–20

Say the name of each picture. Fill in the missing letter for each word.

n ___ t

f ___ x

s ___ n

sh ___ p

cl ___ ck

cr ___ b

NAME ____________________

Lesson 21 Rhyming Words

Color the pictures that rhyme with **bat**  .

NAME ____________________

Lesson 21 Rhyming Words

Draw a line between the rhyming pictures, like **pig**  and **wig**  .

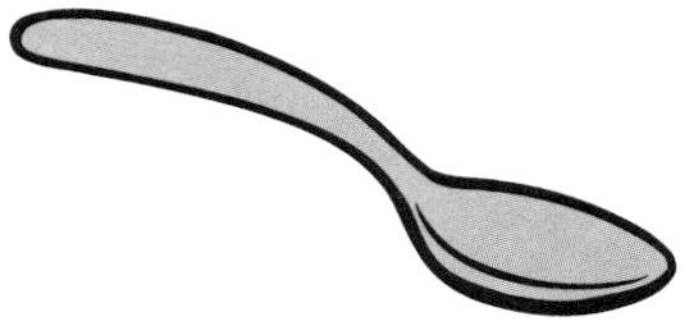

NAME ______________________

Lesson 21 Rhyming Words

Circle the pictures in each row that rhyme with the first picture.

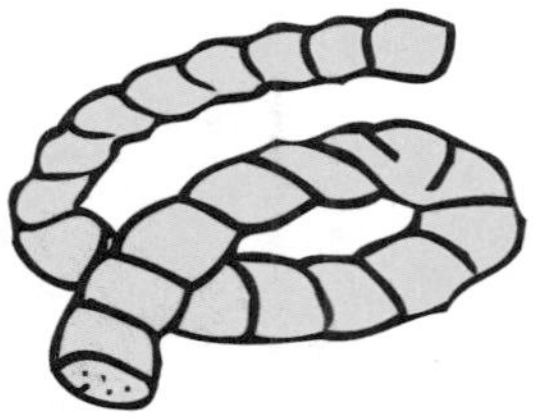

NAME ____________________

Lesson 21 Rhyming Words

Fill in the missing letters for each pair of rhymes.

clock  l______ 

frog  d______ 

top  m______ 

box  f______ 

snow  b______ 

NAME ______________________

Review Lesson 21

Say each picture name. In the box, draw a picture of a rhyming word.

	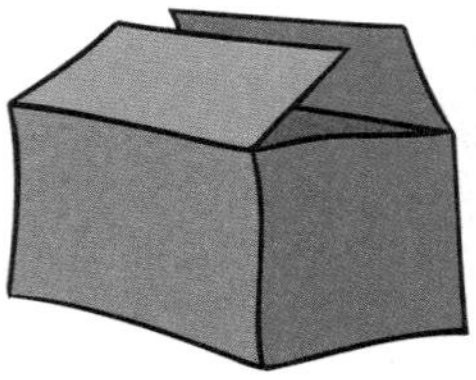
	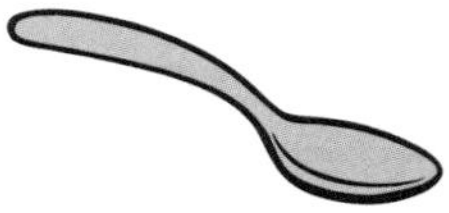

NAME ____________________

Review Lesson 21

Finish each rhyme. Use the words in the box.

red	**truck**	**box**	**pig**

a duck ________

a ________ wig

a fox ________

a ________ bed

LESSON 21 REVIEW

NAME ______________________

Lesson 22 Color Words

Draw a line to match the word with the color.

red

orange

yellow

blue

green

pink

white

black

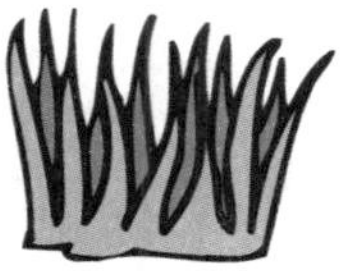

NAME ______________________________

Lesson 22 Color Words

Color each balloon to match the color name.

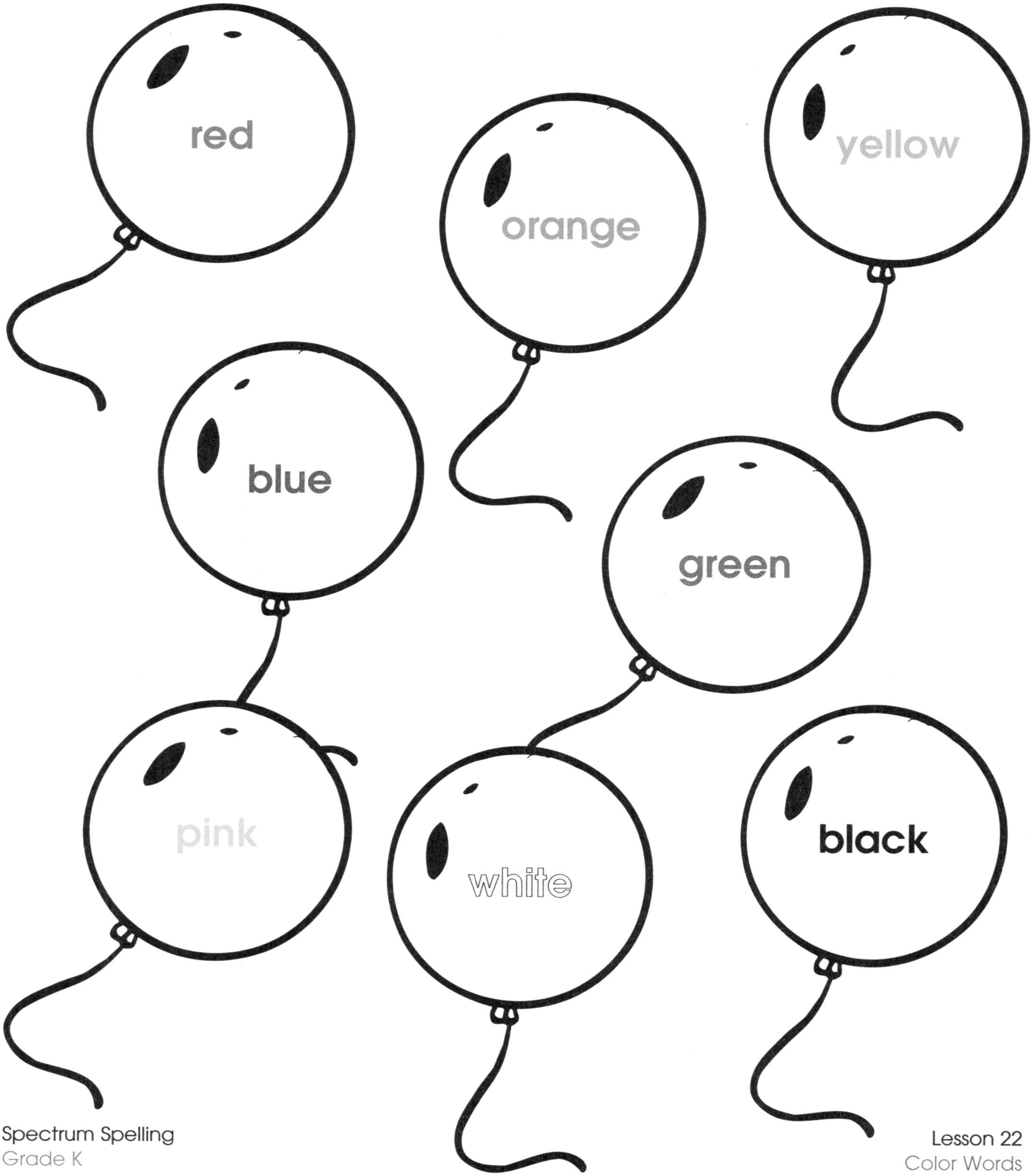

NAME ____________________

Lesson 23 Number Words

Trace the number word. Write it on the line. Then, match the number word to the correct group of animals.

one ____________________

two ____________________

three ____________________

four ____________________

five ____________________

NAME ______________________________

Lesson 23 Number Words

Trace the number word. Write it on the line. Then, match the number word to the correct group of animals.

six ______________________

seven ______________________

eight ______________________

nine ______________________

ten ______________________

NAME ____________________

Lesson 24 Body Words

Fill in the missing letters in the body words. Use the words in the box to help you.

head	hand	foot	arm	leg	chest

___ead

ar___

ches___

han___

___eg

___oot

NAME ____________________

Lesson 24 Body Words

Circle the word that matches each picture.

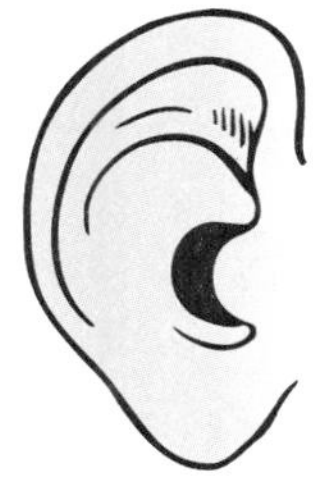

ant **ear**

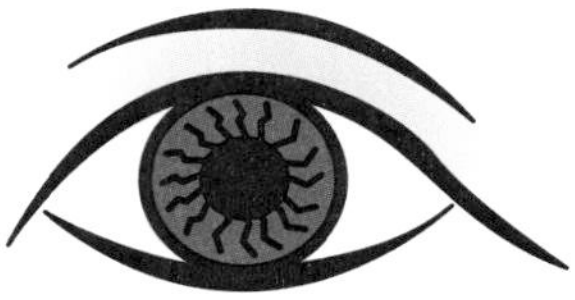

eye **elephant**

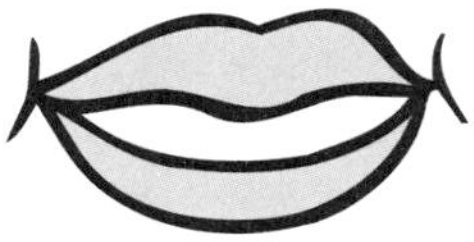

mug **mouth**

nose **nest**

chin **pin**

pan **hair**

NAME ____________________

Review Lessons 22–24

Help the bear find his pot of honey. Follow the number words through the maze. Use the words in the box to help you.

1 one	2 two	3 three	4 four	5 five
6 six	7 seven	8 eight	9 nine	10 ten

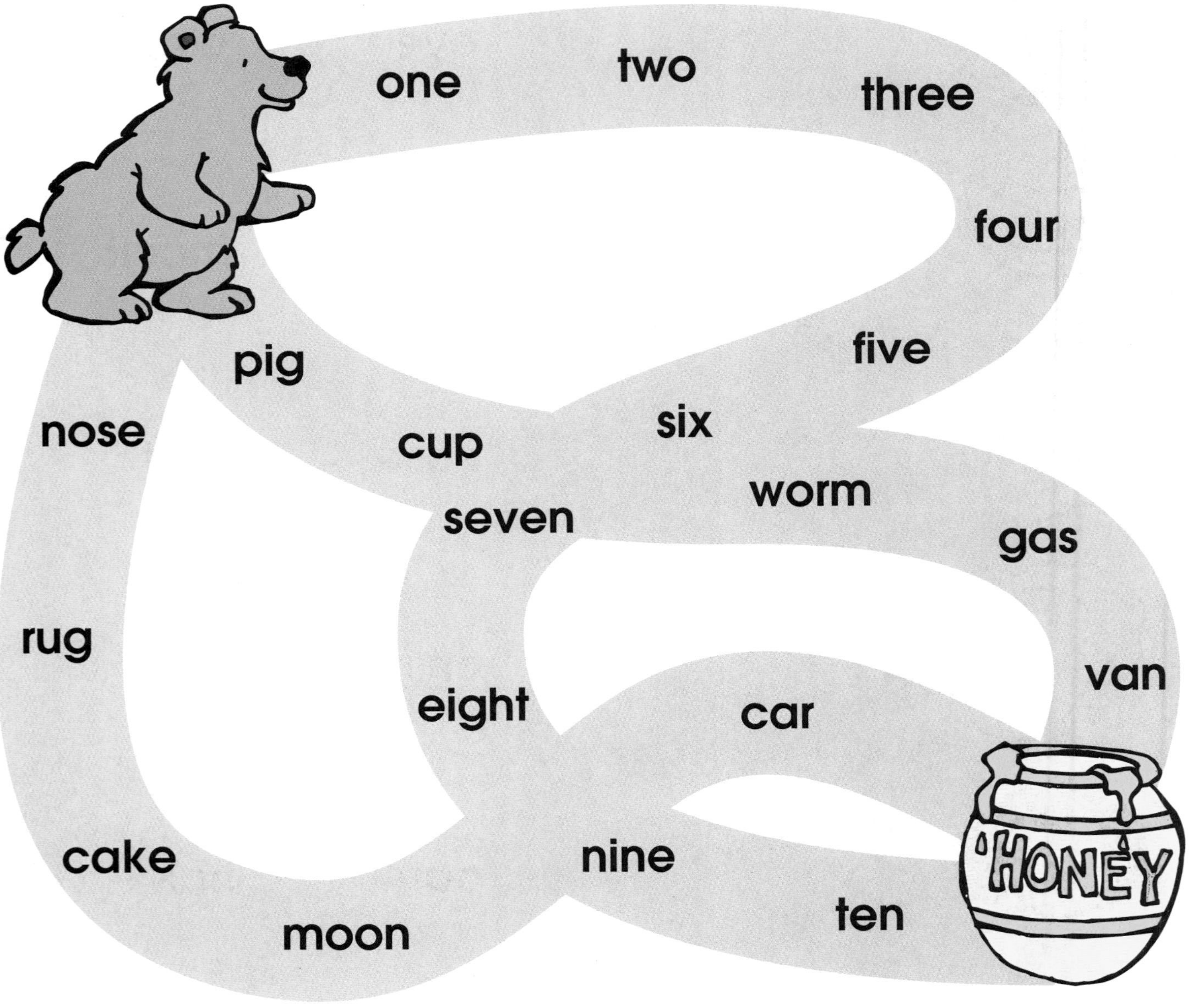

NAME ____________________

Review Lessons 22–24

Trace the body word or color word. Write it on the line. Then, match it to its picture.

pink ____________________

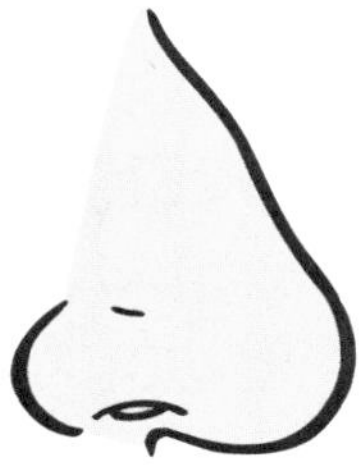

nose ____________________

green ____________________

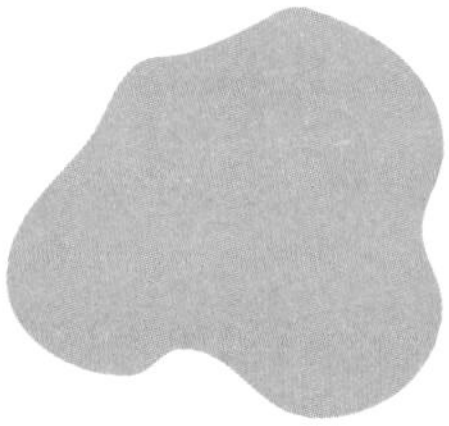

black ____________________

hand ____________________

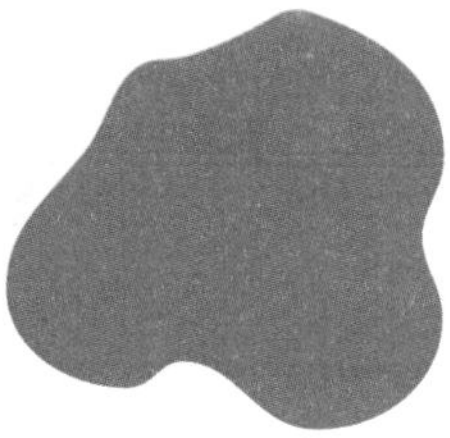

NAME ____________________

Lesson 25 Food Words

Fill in the missing letters in the food words. Use the words in the box to help you.

apple	**juice**	**milk**	**bread**	**peas**	**soup**

___ilk

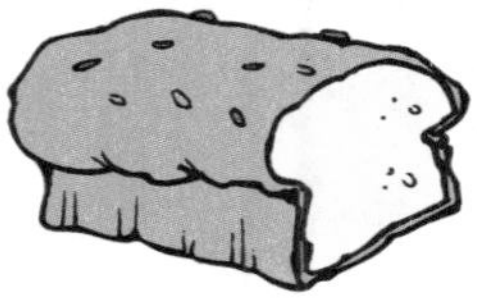

___read

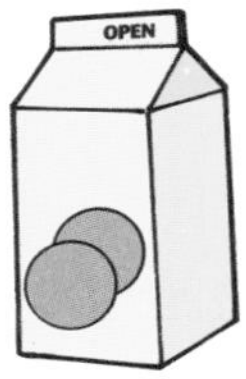

___uice

a___ple

pea___

sou___

NAME ____________________

Lesson 25 Food Words

Draw a line from each word to the food it matches.

milk **apple** **soup** **peas** **bread** **juice**

NAME ____________________

Lesson 26 School Words

Fill in the missing letters in the school words. Use the words in the box to help you.

pen	**paper**	**book**	**desk**	**write**	**read**

__en

pap__r

bo__k

__esk

__rite

rea__

NAME ______________________________

Lesson 26 School Words

Circle the word that matches each picture.

pot pen

paper plug

desk dog

bug book

rock read

write wig

NAME ____________________

Lesson 27 Season Words

Trace the name of each season. Write it on the line. Then, color the picture.

spring

summer

autumn

winter

NAME ______________________

Lesson 27 Season Words

Draw a line to match each picture to the season. Fill in the missing letter in each season. Use the words in the box to help you.

spring	winter	summer	autumn

s __ ring

au __ umn

win __ er

sum __ er

NAME ______________________

Review Lessons 25–27

Choose a season from the box. Draw a picture of that season. Write the season word on the line.

spring	winter	summer	autumn

NAME ______________________

Review Lessons 25–27

The letters in the food words are in the wrong order. Say each picture name. Then, write the correct word on the line.

sopu ______________________

mikl ______________________

pepla ______________________

The letters in the school words are in the wrong order. Say each picture name. Then, write the correct word on the line.

nep ______________________

boko ______________________

dear ______________________

NAME ______________________________

Writing Practice

Use this page to practice writing the ABCs.

Aa Bb Cc Dd Ee Ff Gg Hh Ii Jj Kk Ll Mm
Nn Oo Pp Qq Rr Ss Tt Uu Vv Ww Xx Yy Zz

NAME ______________________

Writing Practice

Use this page to practice writing some words that tell about you.

What is your name? ______________________

How old are you? ______________________

What color are your eyes? ______________________

Do you have a pet? ______________________

What is its name? ______________________

Dictionary

Aa

ant 

apple 

arm 

Bb

ball 

bat 

bed 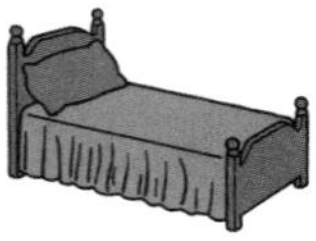

bib 

book 

bus 

Cc

car 

cat 

crab 

cup 

Dd

dog 

doll 

drum 

duck 

Ee

ear 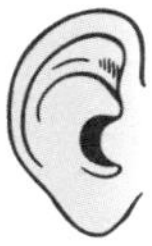

egg 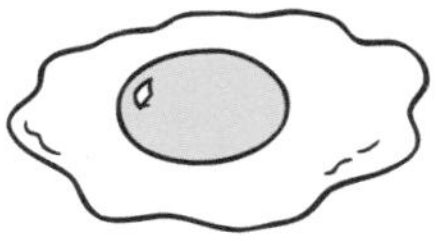

Dictionary

Ff

fan 

fish 

flag 

fox 

frog 

Gg

gas 

goat 

grass 

gum 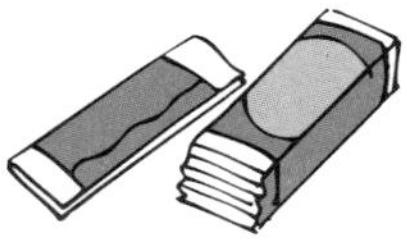

Hh

hand 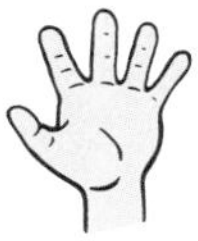

hat 

hen 

Ii

ice cream 

igloo 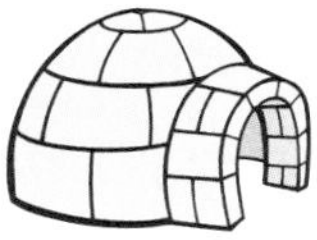

Jj

jam 

jar 

juice 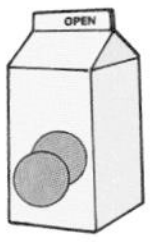

Dictionary

Kk

key 

king 

kite 

Ll

lamp 

leaf 

leg 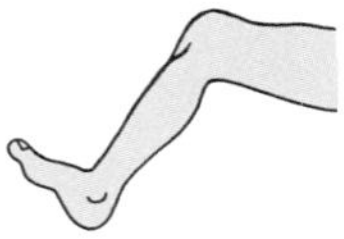

log 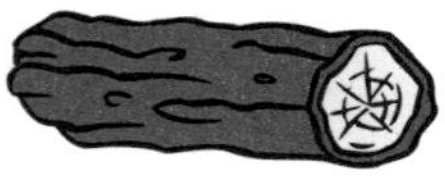

Mm

man 

map 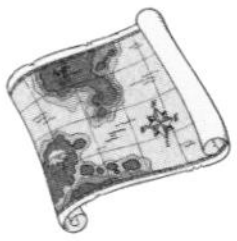

milk 

moon 

mop 

Nn

nail 

nest 

nose 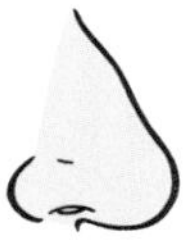

nut 

Oo

octopus 

one 1

owl 

ox 

Pp

pan 

pen 

pig 

pot 

Qq

queen 

Rr

rake 

red 

ring 

rope 

rug 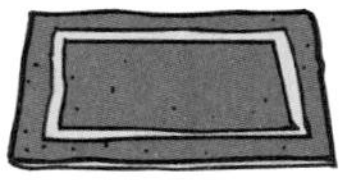

Ss

six 

sled 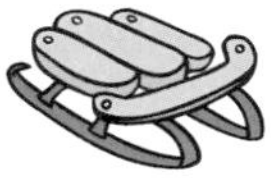

snake 

sock 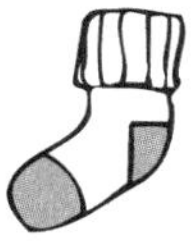

soup 

sun 

Tt

tent 

top 

tree 

tub 

Dictionary

Uu

umbrella 

up 

Vv

van 

vase 

vest 

violin 

Ww

watch 

web 

whale 

Xx

X-ray 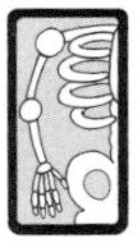

Yy

yarn 

yellow

yo-yo 

Zz

zebra 

zipper 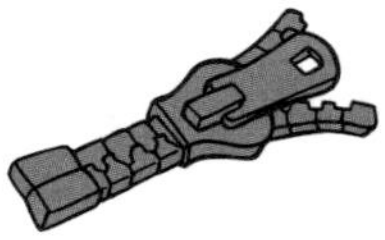

zoo 

Answer Key

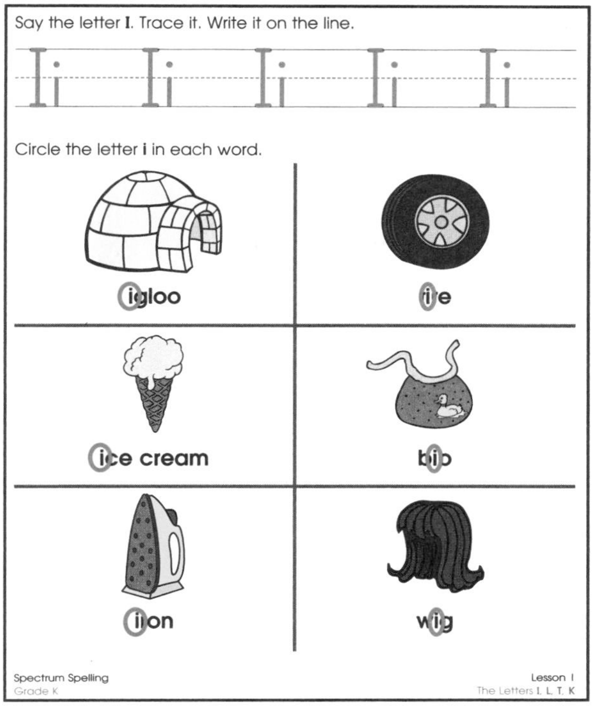
Say the letter **I**. Trace it. Write it on the line.
Ii Ii Ii Ii Ii
Circle the letter **i** in each word.
igloo
tire
ice cream
bib
iron
wig
Spectrum Spelling
Grade K
Lesson 1
The Letters I, L, T, K

6

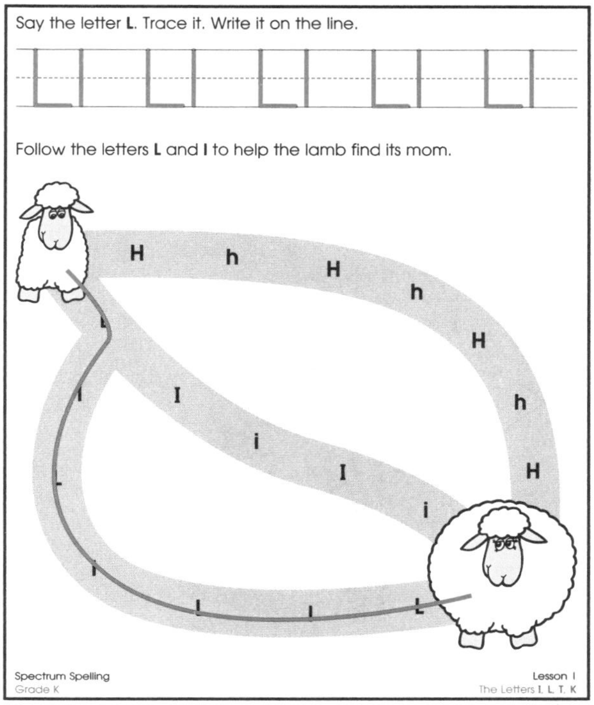
Say the letter **L**. Trace it. Write it on the line.
Ll Ll Ll Ll Ll
Follow the letters **L** and **l** to help the lamb find its mom.
Spectrum Spelling
Grade K
Lesson 1
The Letters I, L, T, K

7

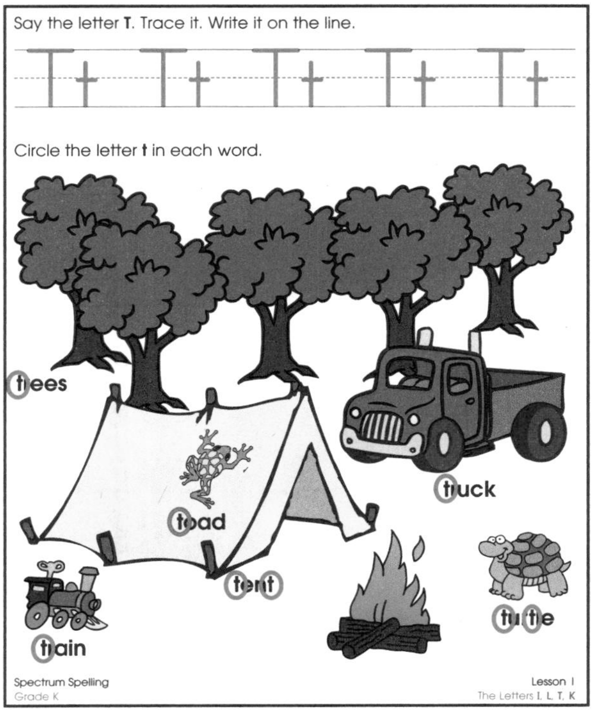
Say the letter **T**. Trace it. Write it on the line.
Tt Tt Tt Tt Tt
Circle the letter **t** in each word.
trees
truck
toad
tent
train
turtle
Spectrum Spelling
Grade K
Lesson 1
The Letters I, L, T, K

8

Say the letter **K**. Trace it. Write it on the line.
Kk Kk Kk Kk Kk
Color the kites with a capital **K** orange. Color the kites with a lowercase **k** blue.
K
K
k
K
k
Spectrum Spelling
Grade K
Lesson 1
The Letters I, L, T, K

9

Answer Key

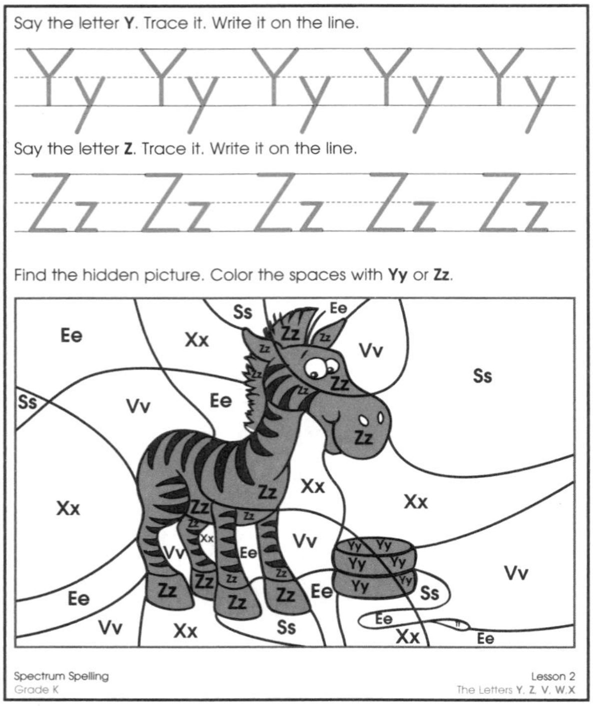
Say the letter **Y**. Trace it. Write it on the line.
Yy Yy Yy Yy Yy
Say the letter **Z**. Trace it. Write it on the line.
Zz Zz Zz Zz Zz
Find the hidden picture. Color the spaces with **Yy** or **Zz**.
Spectrum Spelling
Grade K
Lesson 2
The Letters Y, Z, V, W, X

10

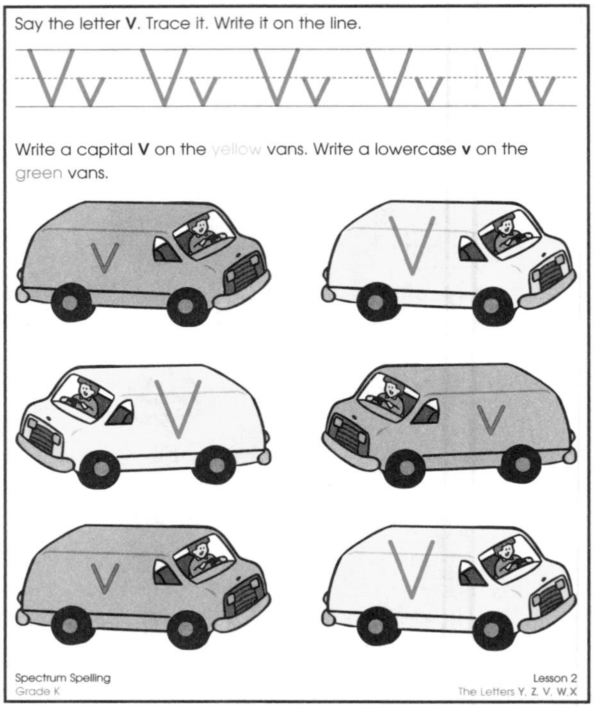
Say the letter **V**. Trace it. Write it on the line.
Vv Vv Vv Vv Vv
Write a capital **V** on the yellow vans. Write a lowercase **v** on the green vans.
Spectrum Spelling
Grade K
Lesson 2
The Letters Y, Z, V, W, X

11

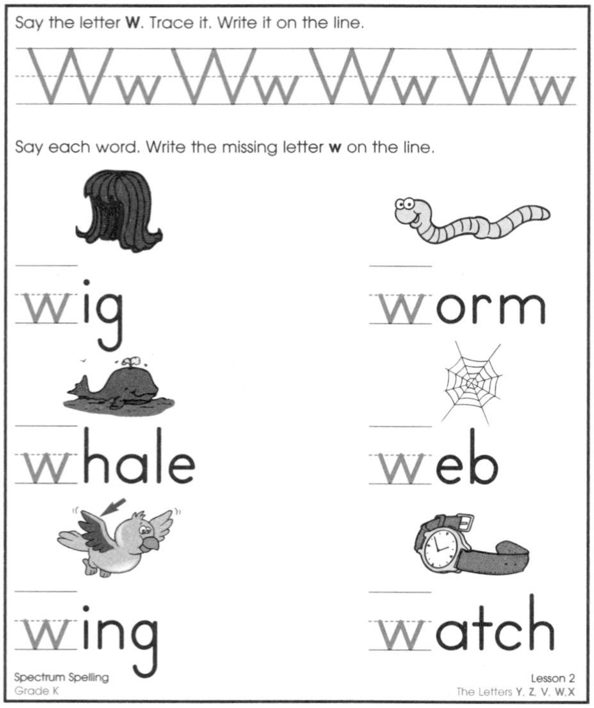
Say the letter **W**. Trace it. Write it on the line.
Ww Ww Ww Ww
Say each word. Write the missing letter **w** on the line.
wig
worm
whale
web
wing
watch
Spectrum Spelling
Grade K
Lesson 2
The Letters Y, Z, V, W, X

12

Say the letter **X**. Trace it. Write it on the line.
Xx Xx Xx Xx Xx
Circle the letter **x** in each word.
fox
ax
six
box
X-ray
ox
Spectrum Spelling
Grade K
Lesson 2
The Letters Y, Z, V, W, X

13

Answer Key

Say the letter **O**. Trace it. Write it on the line.

Oo Oo Oo Oo Oo

Find the hidden picture. Color the spaces with **O** or **o**.

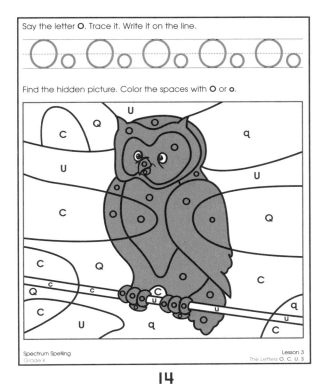

Spectrum Spelling
Grade K

Lesson 3
The Letters **O, C, U, S**

14

Say the letter **C**. Trace it. Write it on the line.

Cc Cc Cc Cc Cc

Say each word. Write the missing letter **c** on the line.

c up

c ow

c ap

c ast

c at

c ut

Spectrum Spelling
Grade K

Lesson 3
The Letters **O, C, U, S**

15

Say the letter **U**. Trace it. Write it on the line.

Uu Uu Uu Uu Uu

Follow the letters **U** and **u** to help the girl find her umbrella.

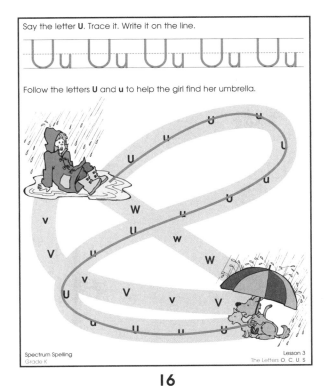

Spectrum Spelling
Grade K

Lesson 3
The Letters **O, C, U, S**

16

Say the letter **S**. Trace it. Write it on the line.

Ss Ss Ss Ss Ss

Circle the letter **s** in each word.

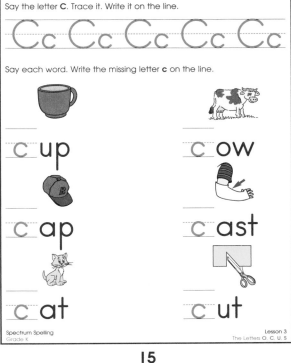

Spectrum Spelling
Grade K

Lesson 3
The Letters **O, C, U, S**

17

Answer Key

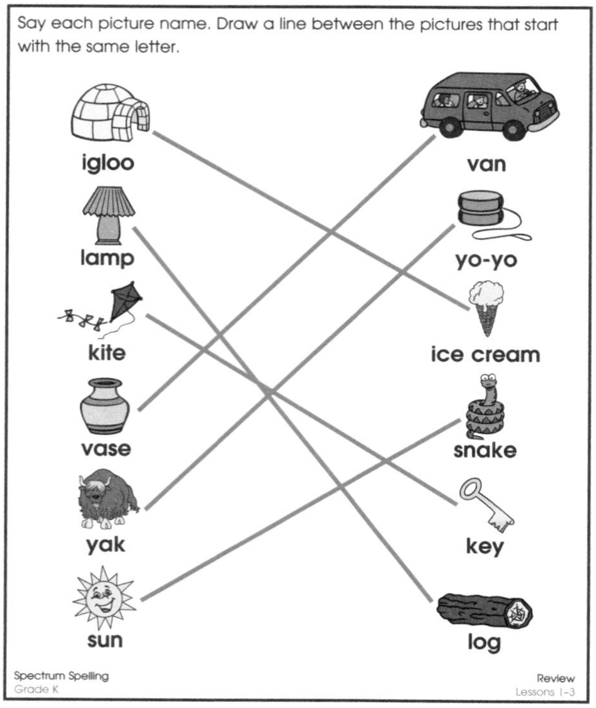
Say each picture name. Draw a line between the pictures that start with the same letter.

igloo — ice cream
lamp — log
kite — key
vase — van
yak — yo-yo
sun — snake

Spectrum Spelling
Grade K
Review
Lessons 1–3

18

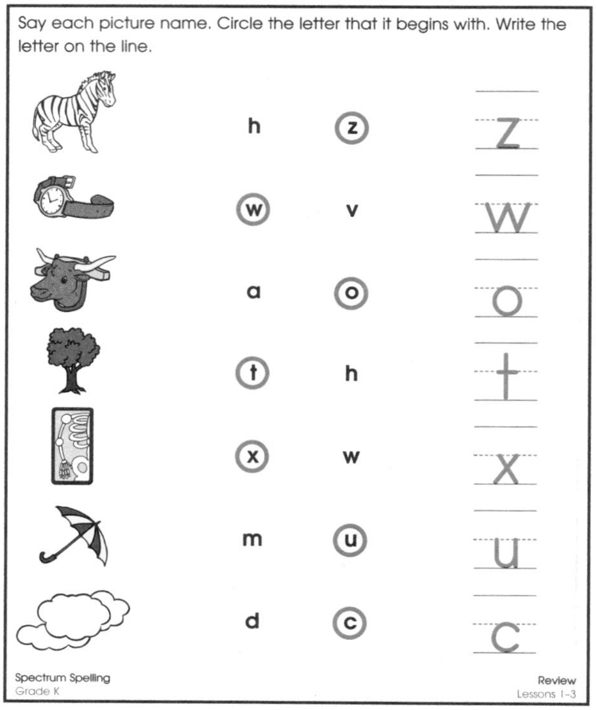
Say each picture name. Circle the letter that it begins with. Write the letter on the line.

h	(z)	z
(w)	v	w
a	(o)	o
(t)	h	t
(x)	w	x
m	(u)	u
d	(c)	c

Spectrum Spelling
Grade K
Review
Lessons 1–3

19

Say the letter **J**. Trace it. Write it on the line.

Jj Jj Jj Jj Jj

Color the jam jars with a capital **J** red. Color the jam jars with a lowercase **j** purple.

J j j
J J
j J j

Spectrum Spelling
Grade K
Lesson 4
The Letters J, G, P, B

20

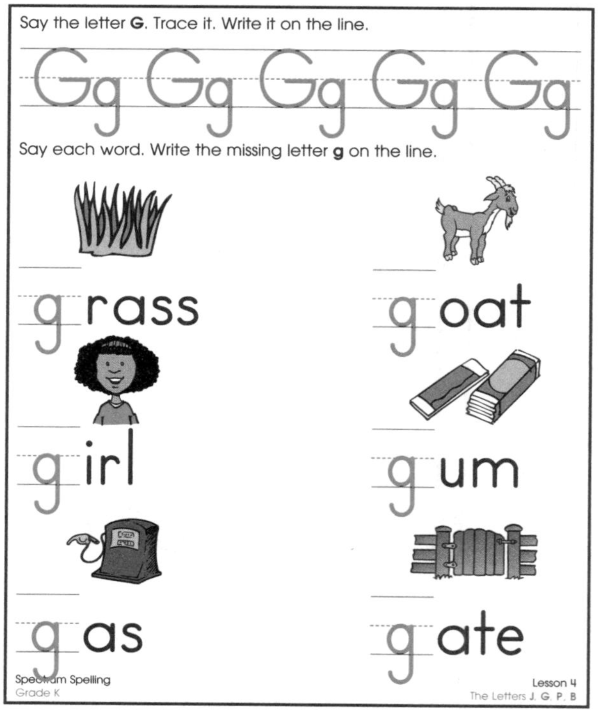
Say the letter **G**. Trace it. Write it on the line.

Gg Gg Gg Gg Gg

Say each word. Write the missing letter **g** on the line.

grass goat
girl gum
gas gate

Spectrum Spelling
Grade K
Lesson 4
The Letters J, G, P, B

21

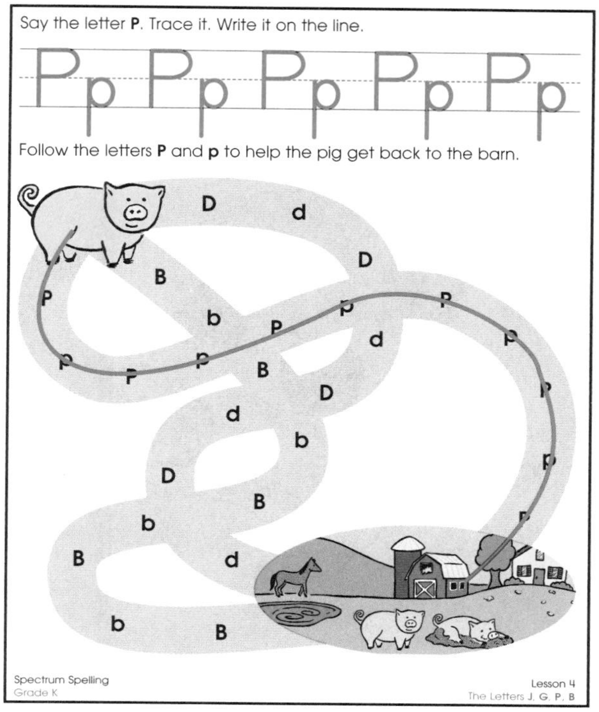

Say the letter **P**. Trace it. Write it on the line.

Pp Pp Pp Pp Pp

Follow the letters **P** and **p** to help the pig get back to the barn.

Spectrum Spelling
Grade K

Lesson 4
The Letters J, G, P, B

22

Say the letter **B**. Trace it. Write it on the line.

Bb Bb Bb Bb Bb

Circle the letter **b** in each word.

bus
boots
bell
book
bat
bug

Spectrum Spelling
Grade K

Lesson 4
The Letters J, G, P, B

23

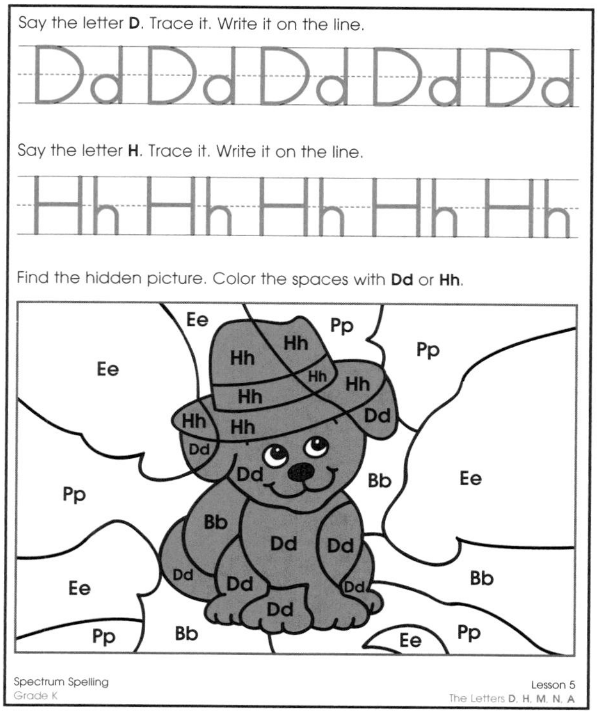

Say the letter **D**. Trace it. Write it on the line.

Dd Dd Dd Dd Dd

Say the letter **H**. Trace it. Write it on the line.

Hh Hh Hh Hh Hh

Find the hidden picture. Color the spaces with **Dd** or **Hh**.

Spectrum Spelling
Grade K

Lesson 5
The Letters D, H, M, N, A

24

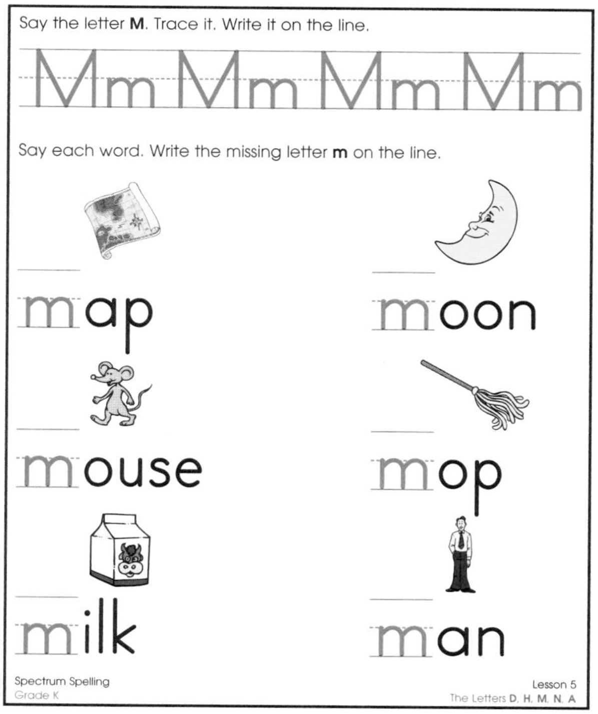

Say the letter **M**. Trace it. Write it on the line.

Mm Mm Mm Mm

Say each word. Write the missing letter **m** on the line.

map
moon
mouse
mop
milk
man

Spectrum Spelling
Grade K

Lesson 5
The Letters D, H, M, N, A

25

Answer Key

Say the letter **N**. Trace it. Write it on the line.

Nn Nn Nn Nn Nn

Find the hidden picture. Color the spaces with **N** or **n**.

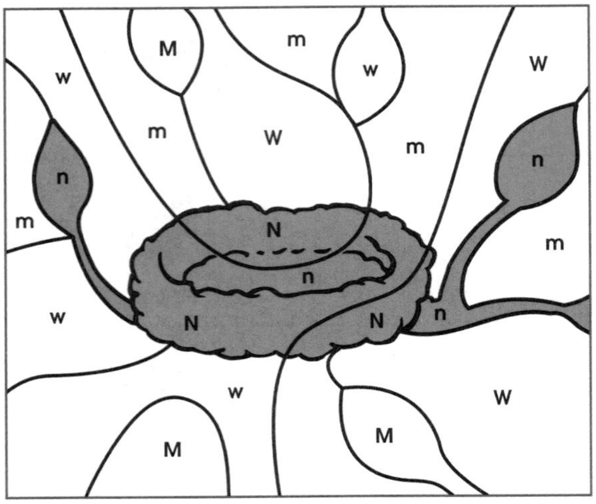

Spectrum Spelling
Grade K

Lesson 5
The Letters D, H, M, N, A

26

Say the letter **A**. Trace it. Write it on the line.

Aa Aa Aa Aa Aa

Color the apples with a capital **A** red. Color the apples with a lowercase **a** green.

Spectrum Spelling
Grade K

Lesson 5
The Letters D, H, M, N, A

27

Say the letter **E**. Trace it. Write it on the line.

Ee Ee Ee Ee Ee

Circle the letter **e** in each word.

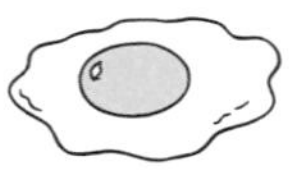
egg

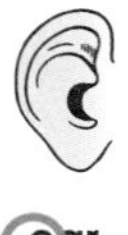
ear

hen

bed

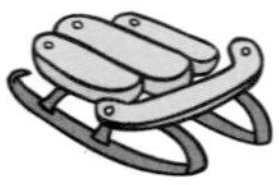
sled

eat

Spectrum Spelling
Grade K

Lesson 6
The Letters E, Q, R, F

28

Say the letter **Q**. Trace it. Write it on the line.

Qq Qq Qq Qq Qq

Follow the letters **Q** and **q** to help the queen find her quilt.

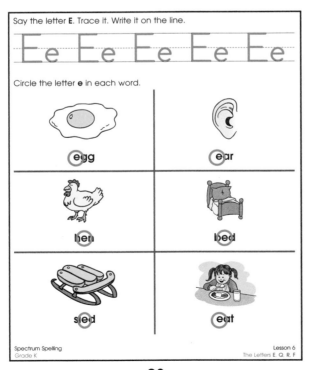

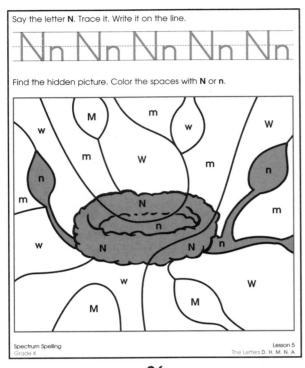

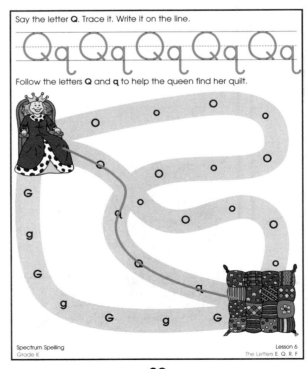

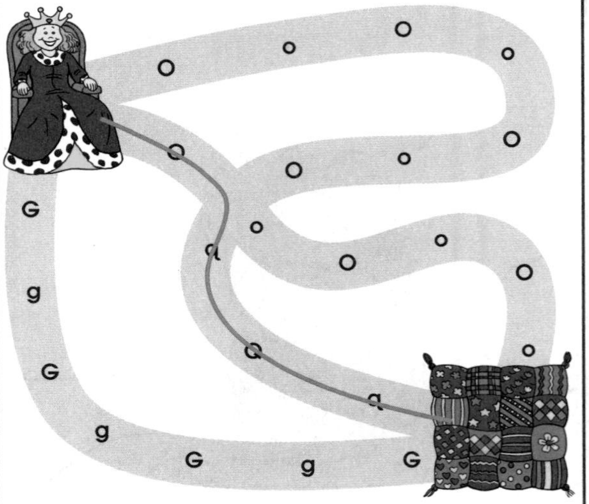

Spectrum Spelling
Grade K

Lesson 6
The Letters E, Q, R, F

29

Answer Key

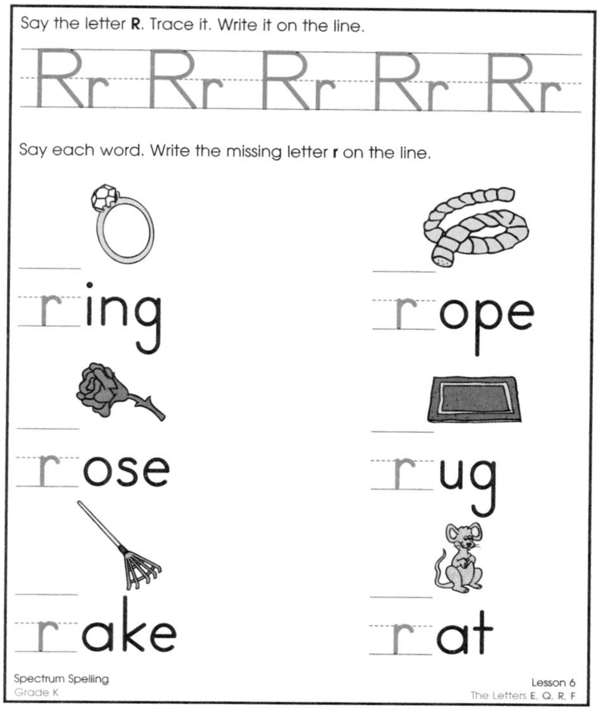

Say the letter **R**. Trace it. Write it on the line.

Rr Rr Rr Rr Rr

Say each word. Write the missing letter **r** on the line.

ring rope

rose rug

rake rat

Spectrum Spelling
Grade K

Lesson 6
The Letters E, Q, R, F

30

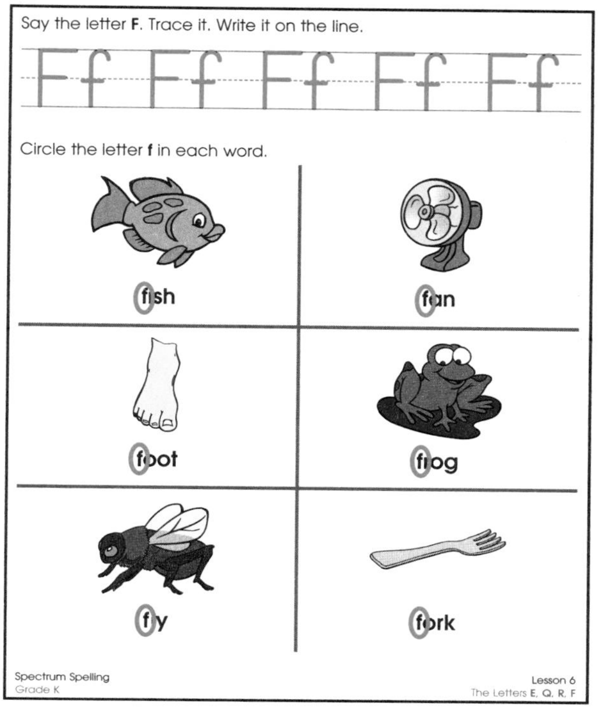

Say the letter **F**. Trace it. Write it on the line.

Ff Ff Ff Ff Ff

Circle the letter **f** in each word.

fish fan

foot frog

fly fork

Spectrum Spelling
Grade K

Lesson 6
The Letters E, Q, R, F

31

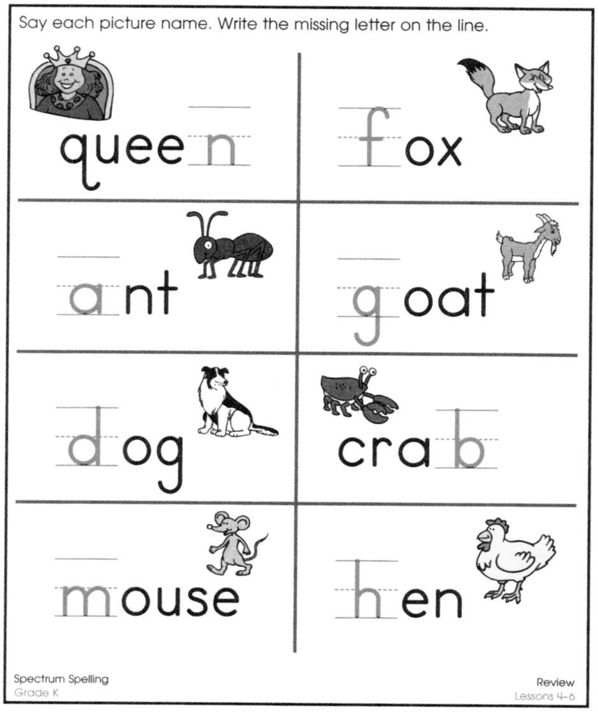

Say each picture name. Write the missing letter on the line.

queen fox

ant goat

dog crab

mouse hen

Spectrum Spelling
Grade K

Review
Lessons 4–6

32

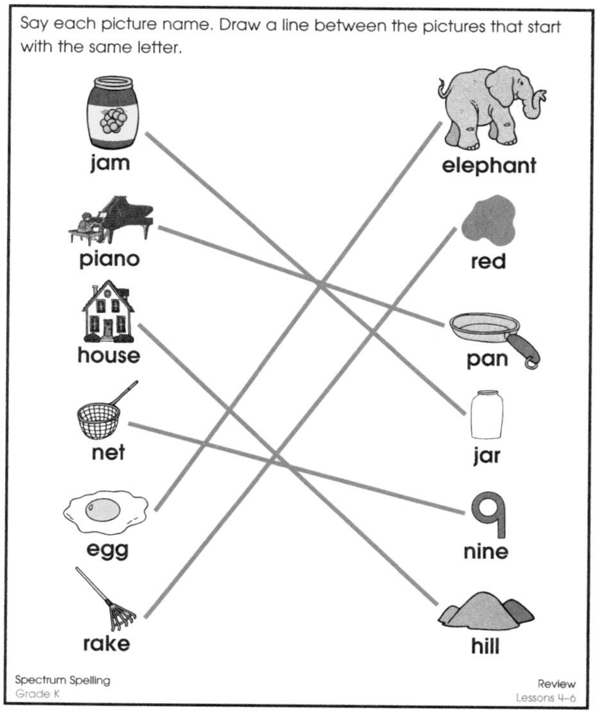

Say each picture name. Draw a line between the pictures that start with the same letter.

jam elephant

piano red

house pan

net jar

egg nine

rake hill

Spectrum Spelling
Grade K

Review
Lessons 4–6

33

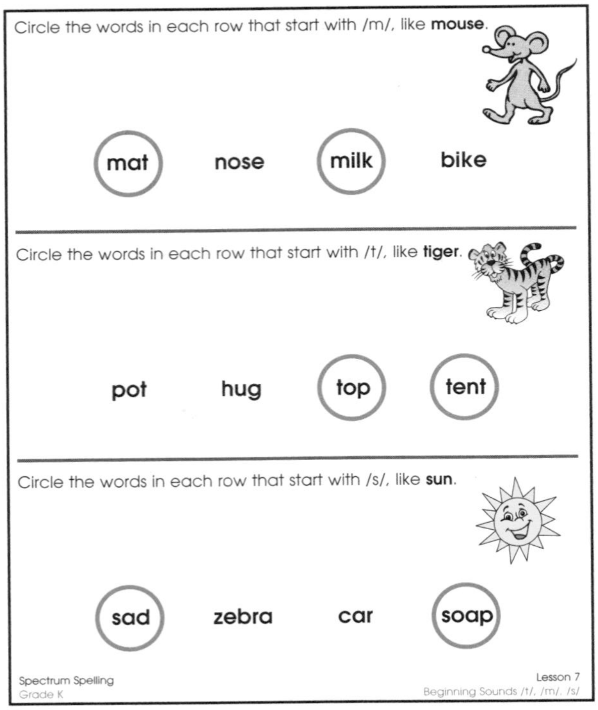
Circle the words in each row that start with /m/, like **mouse**.

mat nose milk bike

Circle the words in each row that start with /t/, like **tiger**.

pot hug top tent

Circle the words in each row that start with /s/, like **sun**.

sad zebra car soap

Spectrum Spelling
Grade K
Lesson 7
Beginning Sounds /t/, /m/, /s/

34

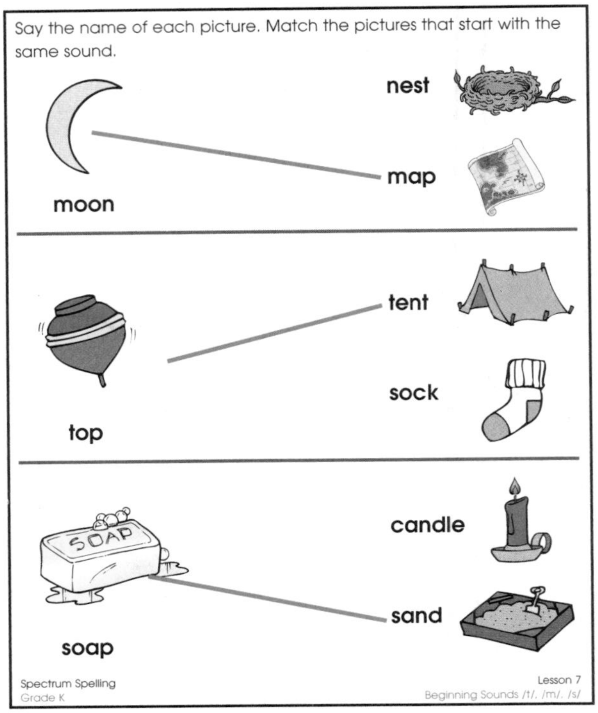
Say the name of each picture. Match the pictures that start with the same sound.

moon — nest — map

top — tent — sock

soap — candle — sand

Spectrum Spelling
Grade K
Lesson 7
Beginning Sounds /t/, /m/, /s/

35

Say the name of each picture. Fill in the missing letter for each word.

feather

jam

dog

cat

fan

Spectrum Spelling
Grade K
Lesson 8
Beginning Sounds /j/, /k/, /d/, /f/

36

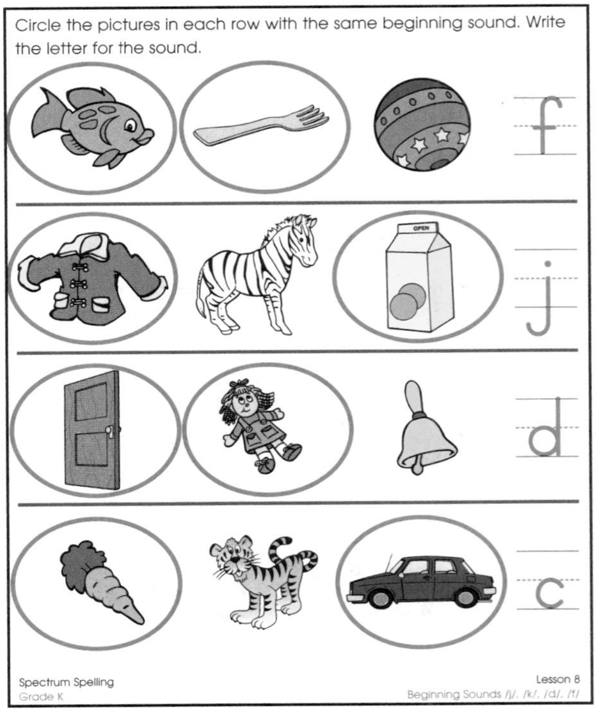
Circle the pictures in each row with the same beginning sound. Write the letter for the sound.

f

j

d

c

Spectrum Spelling
Grade K
Lesson 8
Beginning Sounds /j/, /k/, /d/, /f/

37

Answer Key

Circle the words in each row that start with /k/, like **kite**.
Write the letter **k** on the line.

(king)   hit   ten   (key)   k

Circle the words in each row that start with /d/, like **dog**.
Write the letter **d** on the line.

bed   (dam)   can   (doll)   d

Circle the words in each row that start with /t/, like **turtle**.
Write the letter **t** on the line.

juice   hug   (top)   (train)   t

Say each picture name. Circle the letter for the beginning sound.
Write the letter on the line.

(t)   h   t

t   (f)   f

(s)   c   s

w   (m)   m

y   (j)   j

Circle the words in each row that start with /w/, like **worm**.

(window)   mask   (web)   violin

Circle the words in each row that start with /n/, like **nine**.

mine   (nice)   us   (net)

Circle the words in each row that start with /g/, like **gate**.

queen   (gum)   (game)   yes

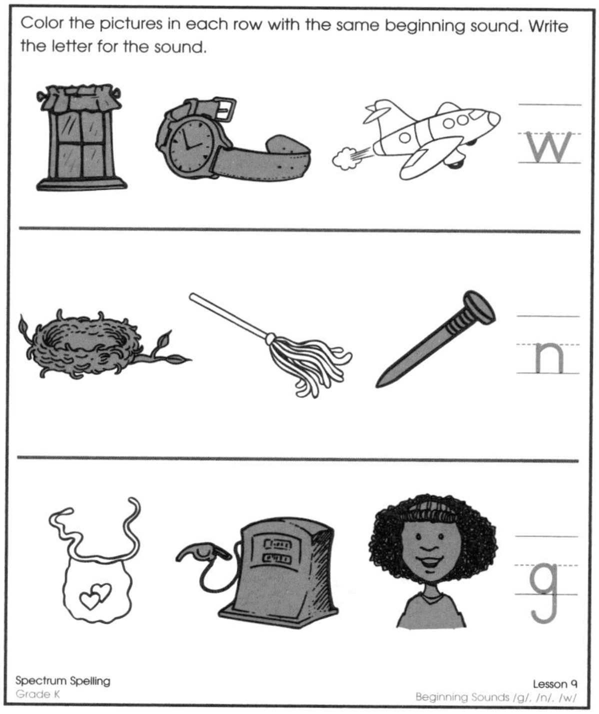

Color the pictures in each row with the same beginning sound. Write
the letter for the sound.

w

n

g

Answer Key

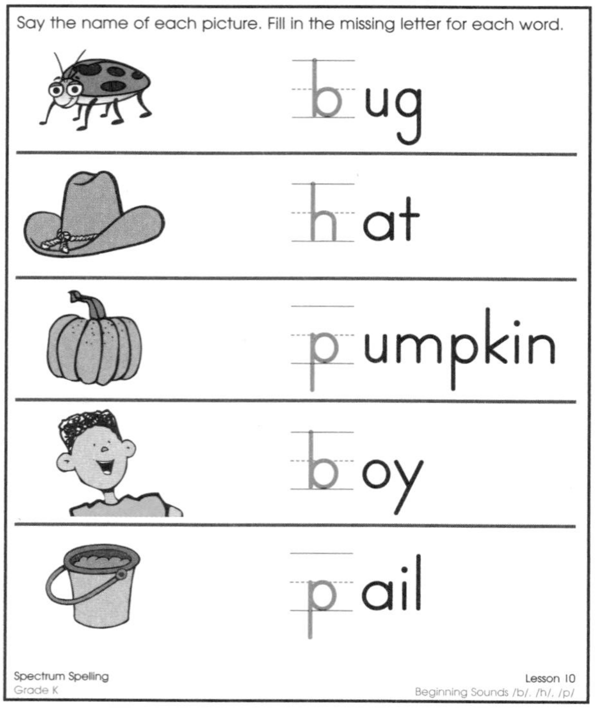
Say the name of each picture. Fill in the missing letter for each word.

b ug

h at

p umpkin

b oy

p ail

Spectrum Spelling
Grade K

Lesson 10
Beginning Sounds /b/, /h/, /p/

42

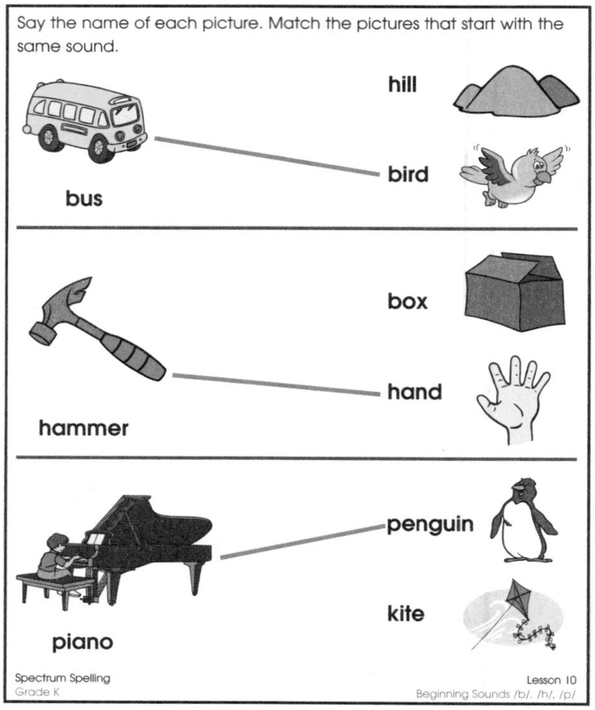
Say the name of each picture. Match the pictures that start with the same sound.

bus — hill, bird

hammer — box, hand

piano — penguin, kite

Spectrum Spelling
Grade K

Lesson 10
Beginning Sounds /b/, /h/, /p/

43

Color each picture that starts with the /w/ sound.

Color each picture that starts with the /p/ sound.

Color each picture that starts with the /b/ sound.

Color each picture that starts with the /g/ sound.

Spectrum Spelling
Grade K

Review
Lessons 9–10

44

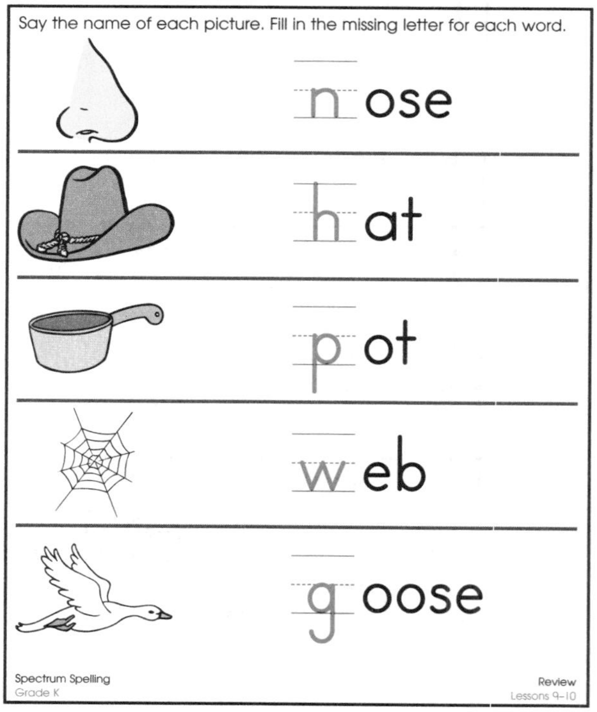
Say the name of each picture. Fill in the missing letter for each word.

n ose

h at

p ot

w eb

g oose

Spectrum Spelling
Grade K

Review
Lessons 9–10

45

Answer Key

Circle the pictures in each row with the same beginning sound. Write the letter for the sound.

l

k

r

Spectrum Spelling
Grade K

Lesson 11
Beginning Sounds /r/, /k/, /l/

46

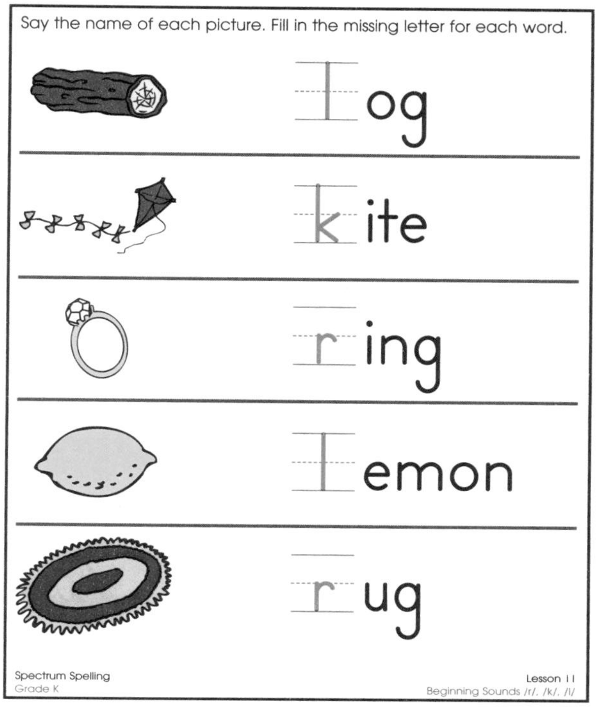
Say the name of each picture. Fill in the missing letter for each word.

log

kite

ring

lemon

rug

Spectrum Spelling
Grade K

Lesson 11
Beginning Sounds /r/, /k/, /l/

47

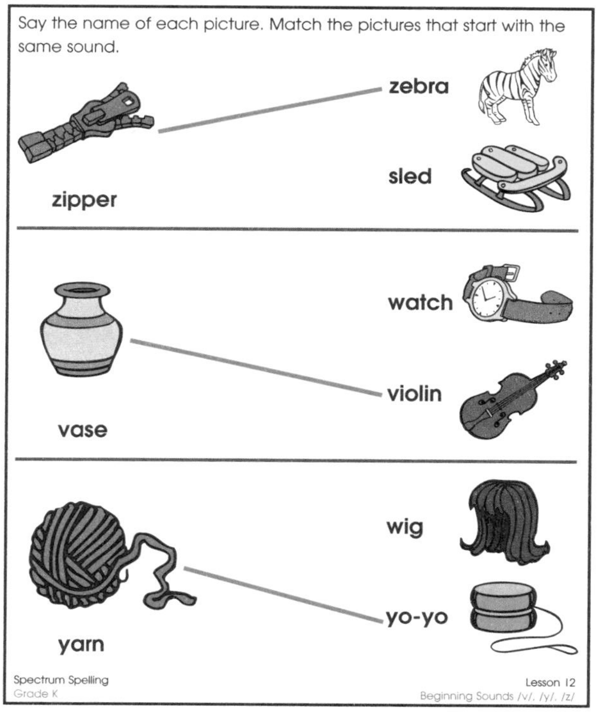
Say the name of each picture. Match the pictures that start with the same sound.

zipper — zebra, sled

vase — watch, violin

yarn — wig, yo-yo

Spectrum Spelling
Grade K

Lesson 12
Beginning Sounds /v/, /y/, /z/

48

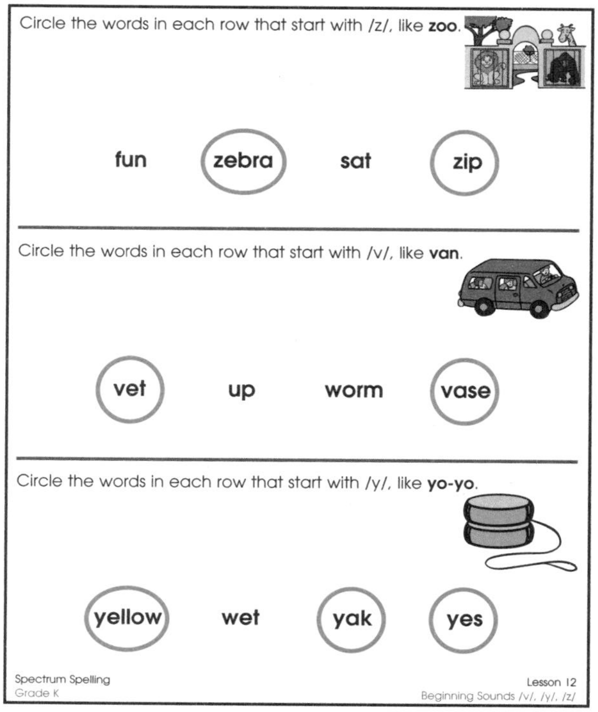
Circle the words in each row that start with /z/, like **zoo**.

fun (zebra) sat (zip)

Circle the words in each row that start with /v/, like **van**.

(vet) up worm (vase)

Circle the words in each row that start with /y/, like **yo-yo**.

(yellow) wet (yak) (yes)

Spectrum Spelling
Grade K

Lesson 12
Beginning Sounds /v/, /y/, /z/

49

Answer Key

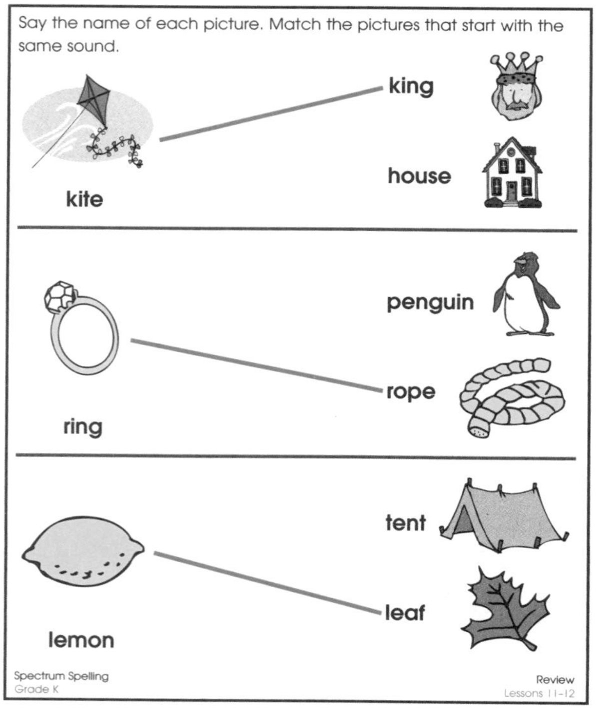
Say the name of each picture. Match the pictures that start with the same sound.

kite — king, house

ring — penguin, rope

lemon — tent, leaf

Spectrum Spelling
Grade K

Review
Lessons 11–12

50

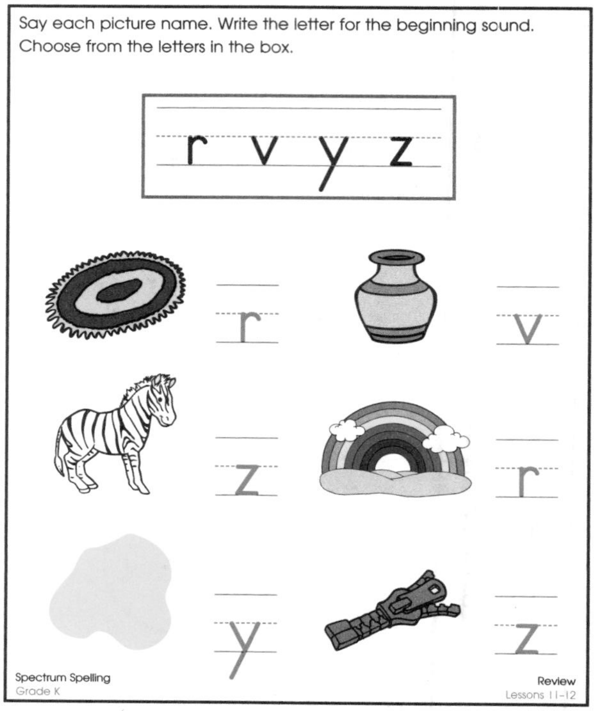
Say each picture name. Write the letter for the beginning sound. Choose from the letters in the box.

r v y z

r v
z r
y z

Spectrum Spelling
Grade K

Review
Lessons 11–12

51

Color each picture that ends with the /d/ sound.

Color each picture that ends with the /t/ sound.

Color each picture that ends with the /m/ sound.

Spectrum Spelling
Grade K

Lesson 13
Ending Sounds /d/, /t/, /m/

52

Say the name of each picture. Fill in the missing letter for each word.

ant swim
red boot
drum cloud

Spectrum Spelling
Grade K

Lesson 13
Ending Sounds /d/, /t/, /m/

53

Answer Key

Circle the words in each row that end with /s/, like **gas**.

sock ship grass mess

Circle the words in each row that end with /g/, like **leg**.

egg lick flag play

Circle the words in each row that end with /b/, like **crab**.

map tub crib hat

Spectrum Spelling
Grade K

Lesson 14
Ending Sounds /s/, /g/, /b/

54

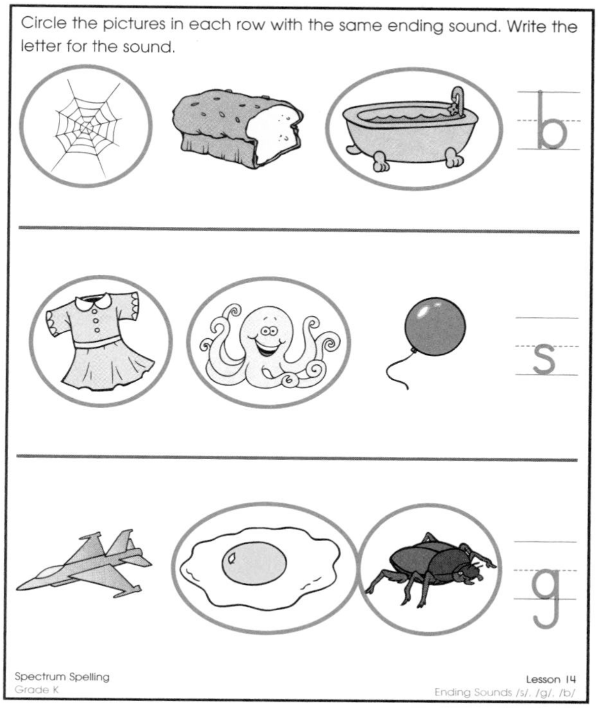

Circle the pictures in each row with the same ending sound. Write the letter for the sound.

b

s

g

Spectrum Spelling
Grade K

Lesson 14
Ending Sounds /s/, /g/, /b/

55

Say the name of each picture. Fill in the missing letter for each word.

clap fox

spoon soup

six queen

Spectrum Spelling
Grade K

Lesson 15
Ending Sounds /p/, /n/, /x/

56

Color each picture that ends with the /p/ sound.

Color each picture that ends with the /n/ sound.

Color each picture that ends with the /x/ sound.

Spectrum Spelling
Grade K

Lesson 15
Ending Sounds /p/, /n/, /x/

57

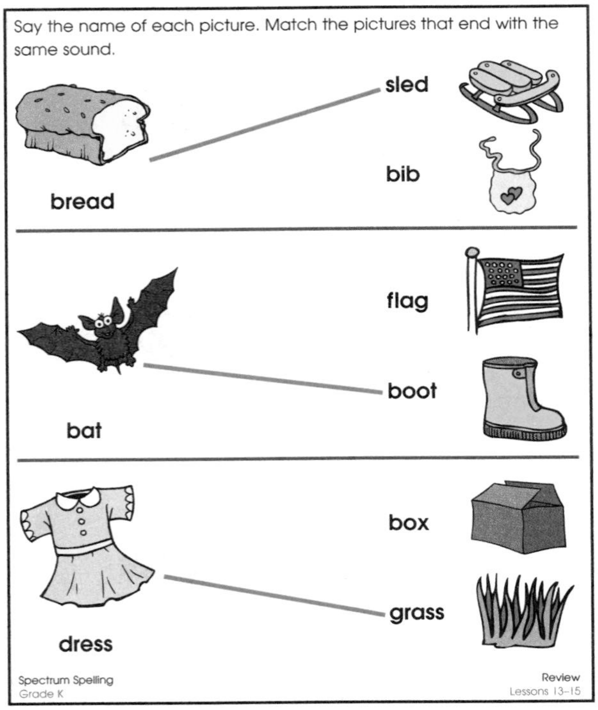

Say the name of each picture. Match the pictures that end with the same sound.

bread — sled

bib

bat — flag

boot

dress — box

grass

Review
Lessons 13–15

58

Say the name of each picture. Fill in the missing letter for each word. Choose from the letters in the box.

m x p g b n

cu p   eg g

o x   lio n

tu b   broo m

Review
Lessons 13–15

59

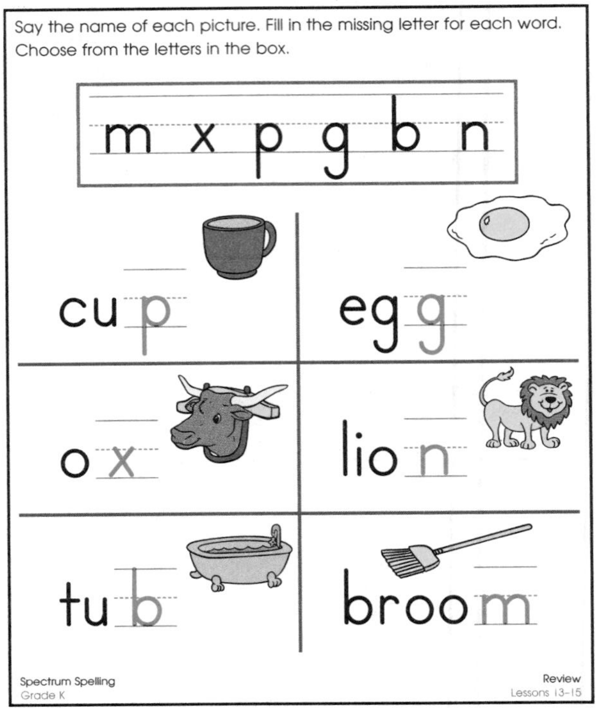

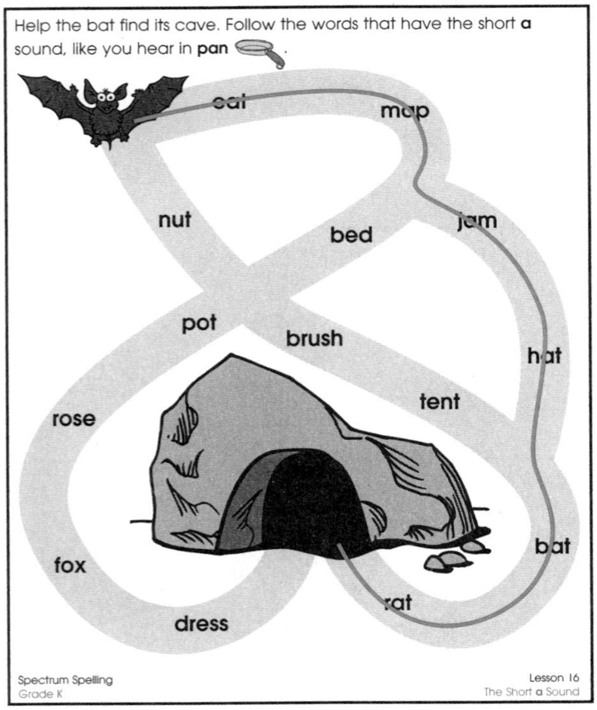

Help the bat find its cave. Follow the words that have the short **a** sound, like you hear in **pan**.

Lesson 16
The Short a Sound

60

Say the name of each picture. Fill in the missing letter for each word.

m a sk   l a mp

c a p   p a n

b a g   f a n

Lesson 16
The Short a Sound

61

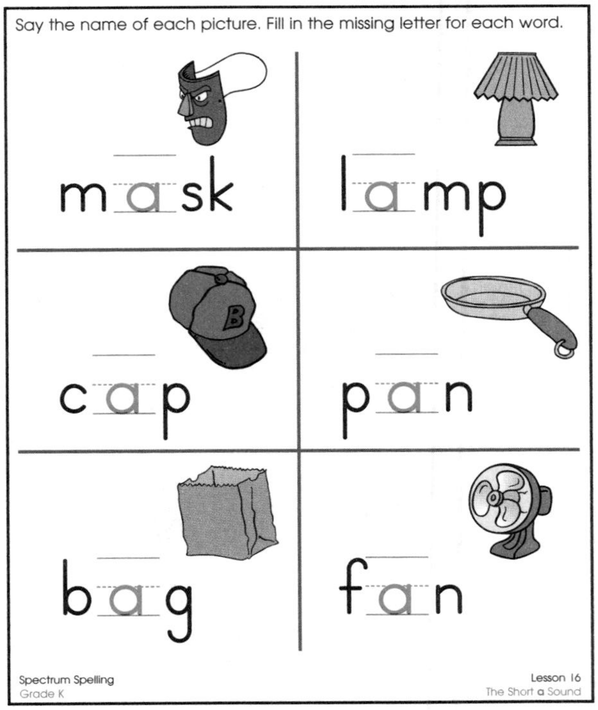

Answer Key

Say the name of each picture. Circle the pictures that have the short **e** sound, like you hear in **dress**

Spectrum Spelling
Grade K

Lesson 17
The Short e Sound

62

Draw a line to match the pictures to the words. In each word, circle the short **e** sound, like you hear in **egg**.

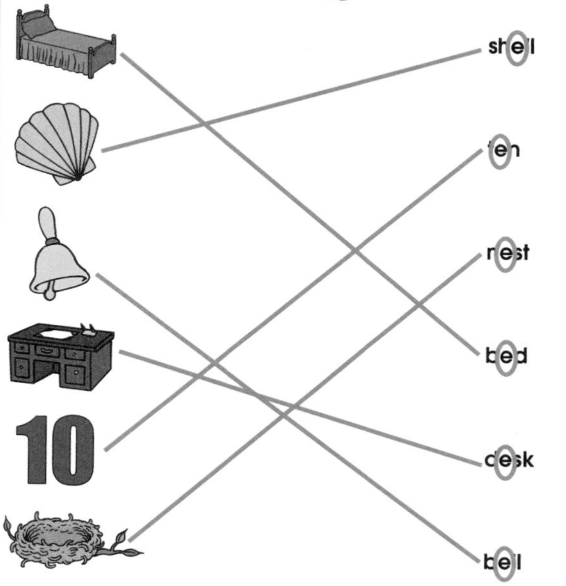

sh(e)ll

t(e)n

n(e)st

b(e)d

d(e)sk

b(e)ll

Spectrum Spelling
Grade K

Lesson 17
The Short e Sound

63

Say each picture name. Circle the pictures that have the short **e** sound, like you hear in **ten 10**.

Cross out the pictures that have the short **a** sound, like you hear in **pan**.

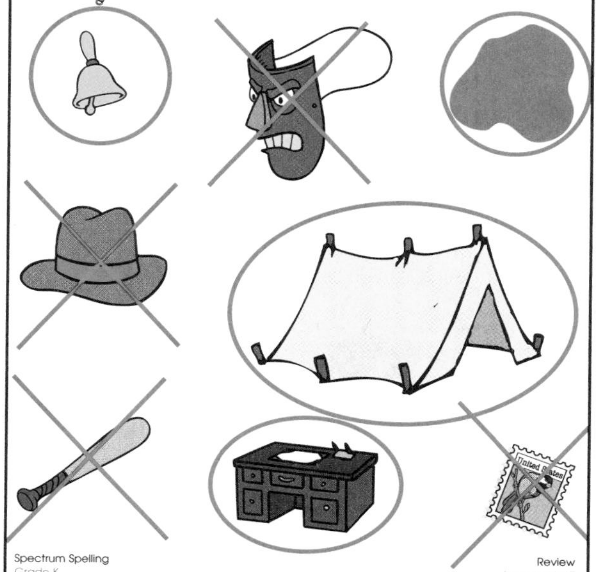

Spectrum Spelling
Grade K

Review
Lessons 16–17

64

Say each picture name. Circle the vowel sound you hear in each word. Circle **a** for the sound you hear in **apple**.

Circle **e** for the sound you hear in **hen**.

(e) a

e (a)

(e) a

e (a)

e (a)

(e) a

Spectrum Spelling
Grade K

Review
Lessons 16–17

65

Spectrum Spelling
Grade K

Answer Key

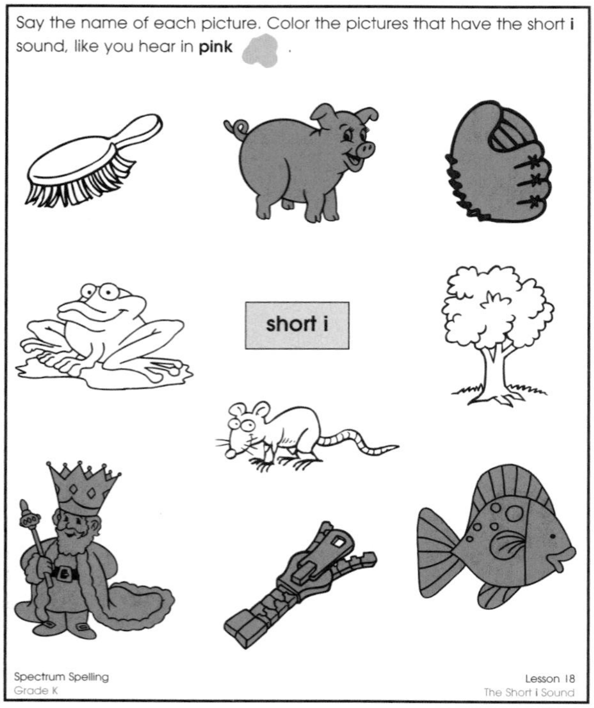

Say the name of each picture. Color the pictures that have the short **i** sound, like you hear in **pink** .

short i

Spectrum Spelling
Grade K

Lesson 18
The Short i Sound

66

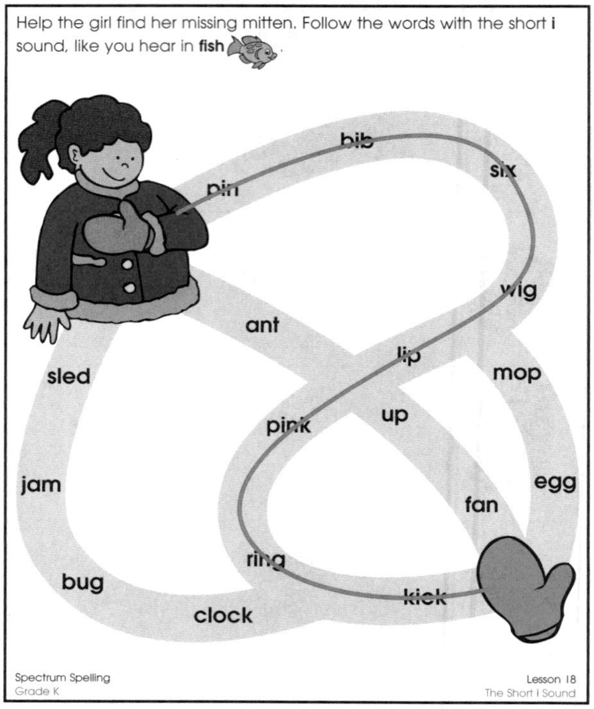

Help the girl find her missing mitten. Follow the words with the short **i** sound, like you hear in **fish** .

Spectrum Spelling
Grade K

Lesson 18
The Short i Sound

67

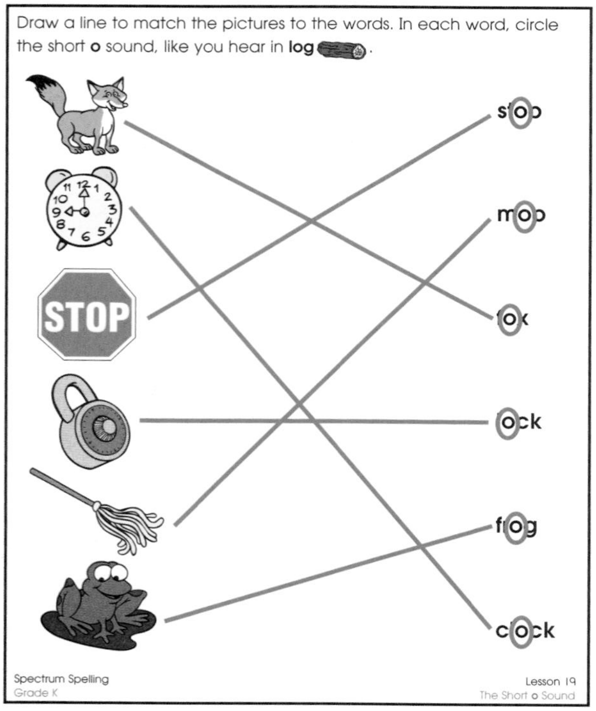

Draw a line to match the pictures to the words. In each word, circle the short **o** sound, like you hear in **log** .

s(o)op
m(o)p
f(o)x
(o)ck
f(o)g
c(o)ck

Spectrum Spelling
Grade K

Lesson 19
The Short o Sound

68

Say the name of each picture. Fill in the missing letter for each word.

t o p   h o t

b o x   s o ck

p o p   bl o cks

Spectrum Spelling
Grade K

Lesson 19
The Short o Sound

69

Spectrum Spelling

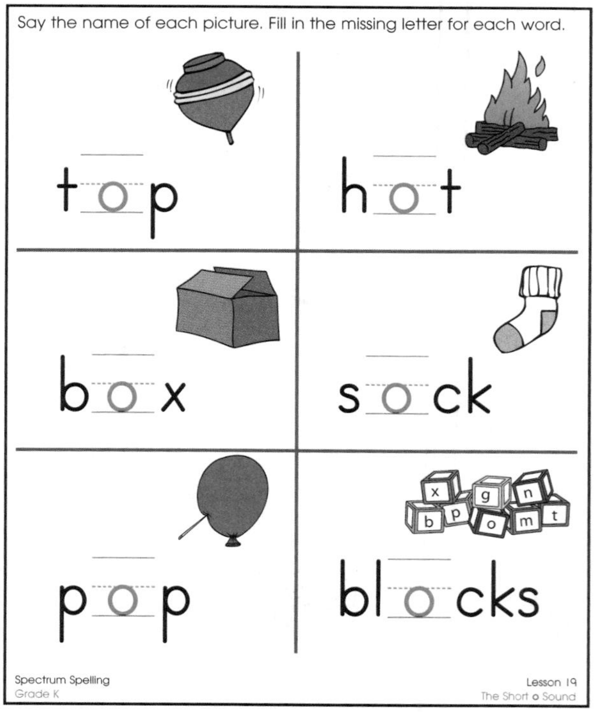

Answer Key

Say the name of each picture. Circle the pictures in each row that have the short **u** sound, like you hear in **cup**.

Spectrum Spelling
Grade K

Lesson 20
The Short **u** Sound

70

Say the name of each picture. Color the pictures that have the short **u** sound, like you hear in **nut**.

Spectrum Spelling
Grade K

Lesson 20
The Short **u** Sound

71

Say the name of each picture. Circle the pictures in each row that have the short **i** sound, like you hear in **pin**.

Say the name of each picture. Circle the pictures in each row that have the short **o** sound, like you hear in **lock**.

Say the name of each picture. Circle the pictures in each row that have the short **u** sound, like you hear in **bug**.

Spectrum Spelling
Grade K

Review
Lessons 18–20

72

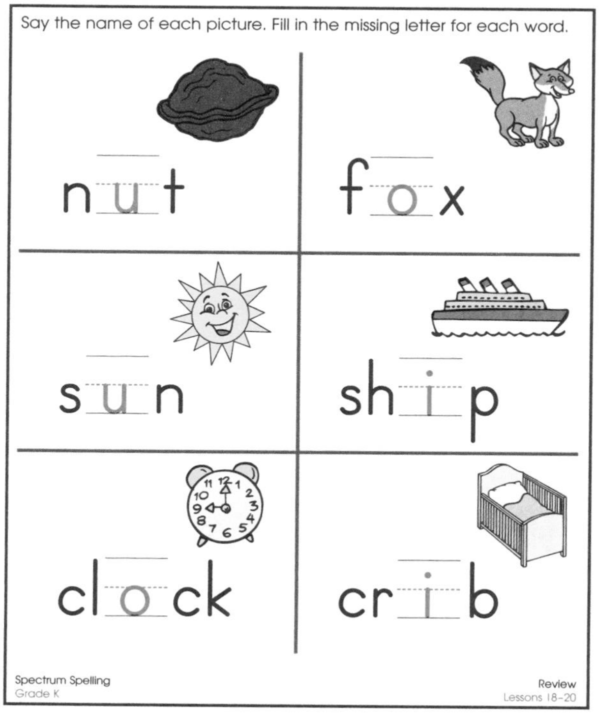

Say the name of each picture. Fill in the missing letter for each word.

Spectrum Spelling
Grade K

Review
Lessons 18–20

73

Answer Key

74

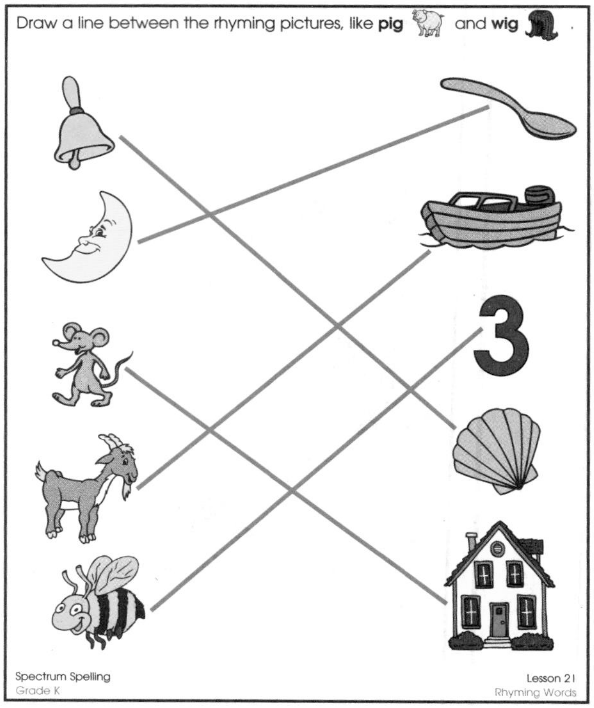

75

76

77

Answer Key

Say each picture name. In the box, draw a picture of a rhyming word.

Possible answer:

Possible answer:

Answers will vary.

Possible answer:

Possible answer:

Spectrum Spelling
Grade K

Review
Lesson 21

78

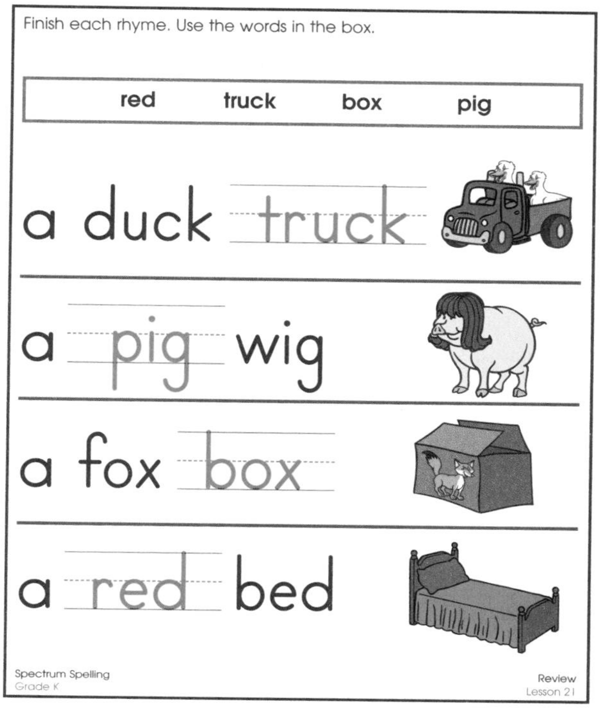
Finish each rhyme. Use the words in the box.

red	truck	box	pig

a duck truck

a pig wig

a fox box

a red bed

Spectrum Spelling
Grade K

Review
Lesson 21

79

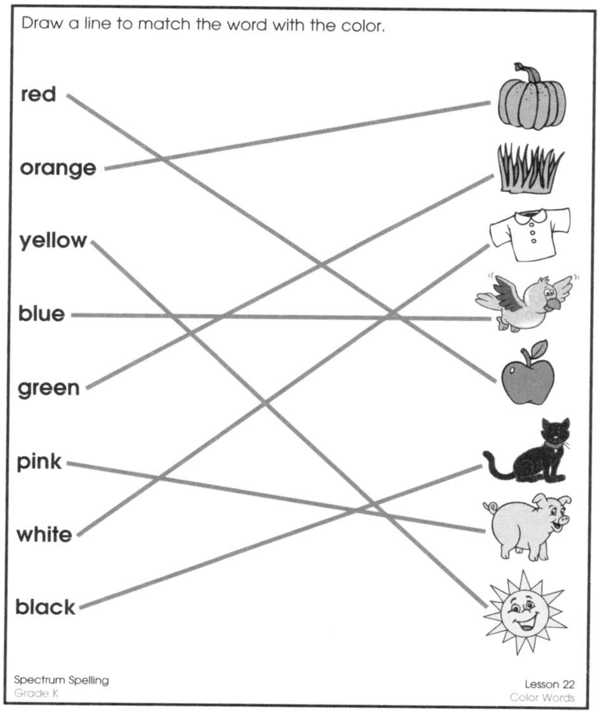
Draw a line to match the word with the color.

red

orange

yellow

blue

green

pink

white

black

Spectrum Spelling
Grade K

Lesson 22
Color Words

80

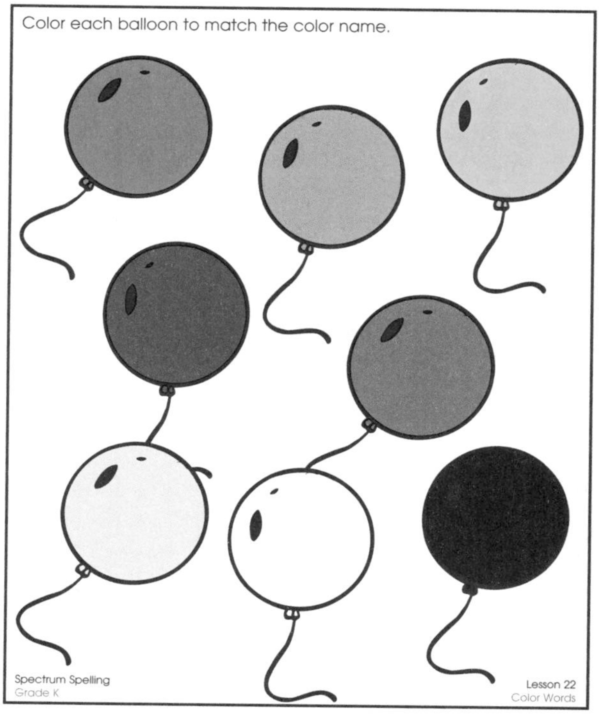
Color each balloon to match the color name.

Spectrum Spelling
Grade K

Lesson 22
Color Words

81

Answer Key

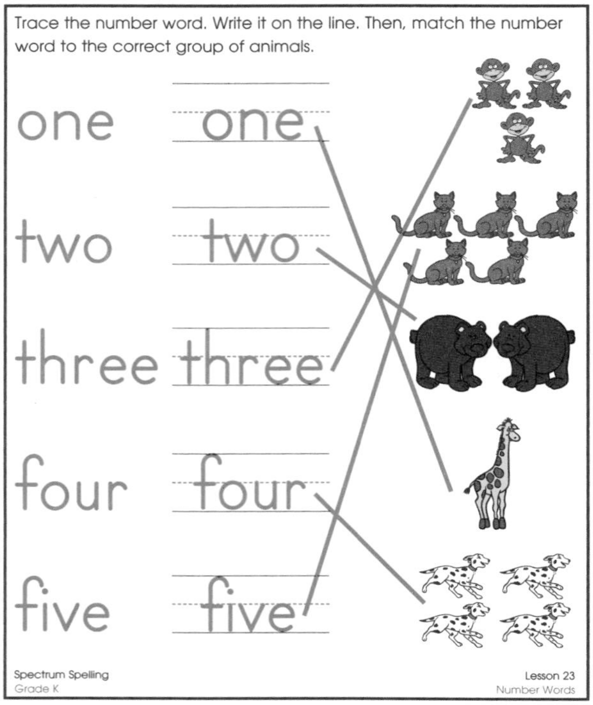

Trace the number word. Write it on the line. Then, match the number word to the correct group of animals.

one one

two two

three three

four four

five five

Spectrum Spelling
Grade K

Lesson 23
Number Words

82

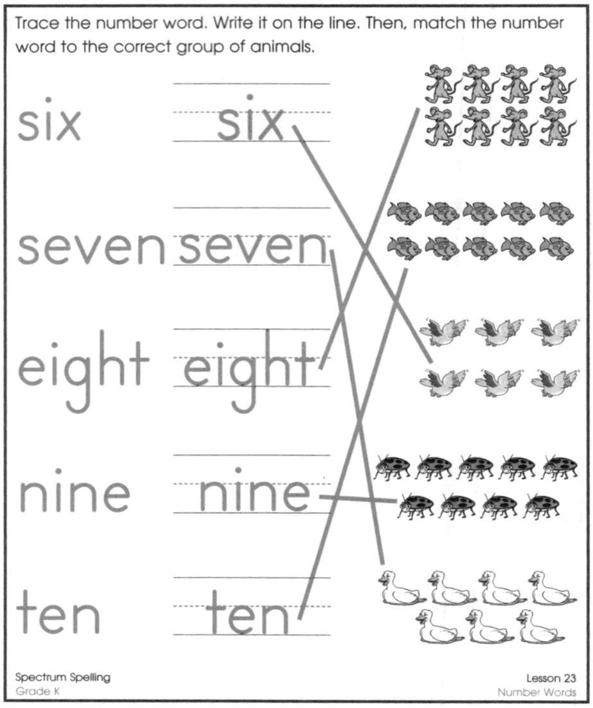

Trace the number word. Write it on the line. Then, match the number word to the correct group of animals.

six six

seven seven

eight eight

nine nine

ten ten

Spectrum Spelling
Grade K

Lesson 23
Number Words

83

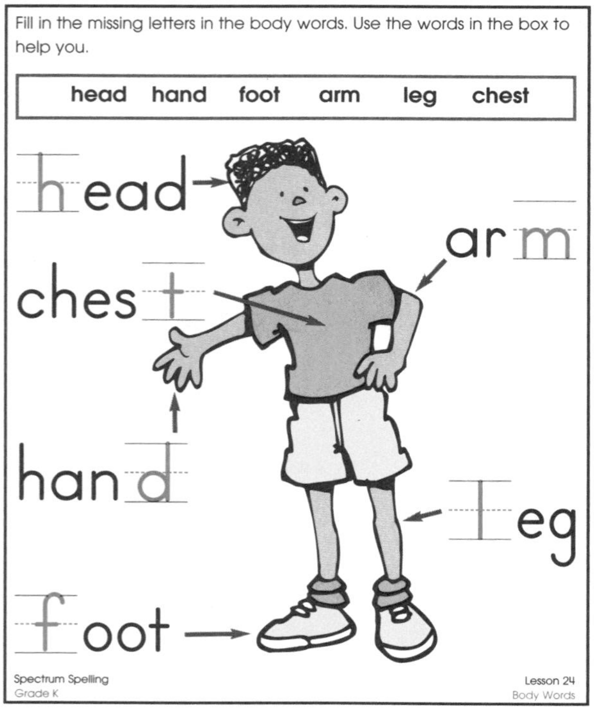

Fill in the missing letters in the body words. Use the words in the box to help you.

head	hand	foot	arm	leg	chest

head

arm

chest

hand

leg

foot

Spectrum Spelling
Grade K

Lesson 24
Body Words

84

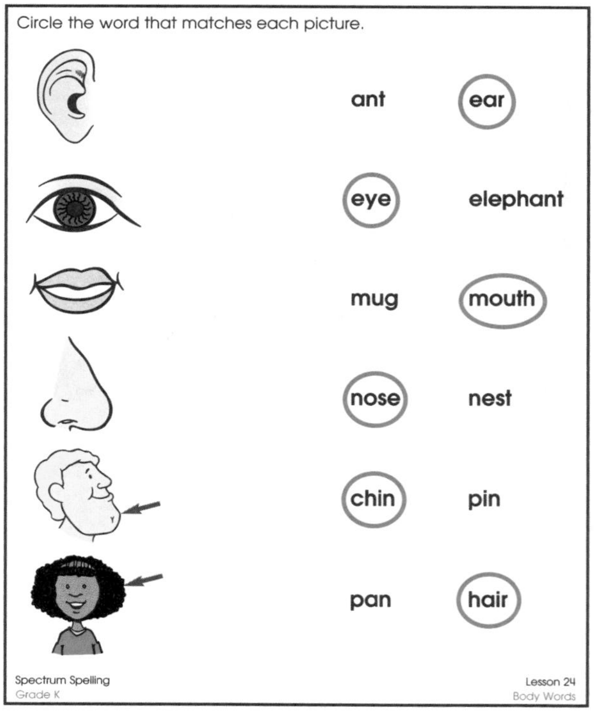

Circle the word that matches each picture.

ant	ear
eye	elephant
mug	mouth
nose	nest
chin	pin
pan	hair

Spectrum Spelling
Grade K

Lesson 24
Body Words

85

Answer Key

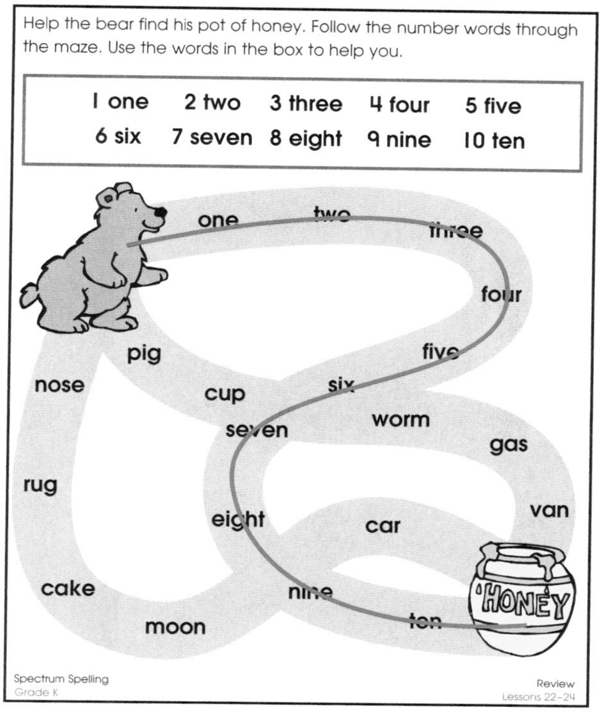
Help the bear find his pot of honey. Follow the number words through the maze. Use the words in the box to help you.

1 one	2 two	3 three	4 four	5 five
6 six	7 seven	8 eight	9 nine	10 ten

Spectrum Spelling
Grade K

Review
Lessons 22–24

86

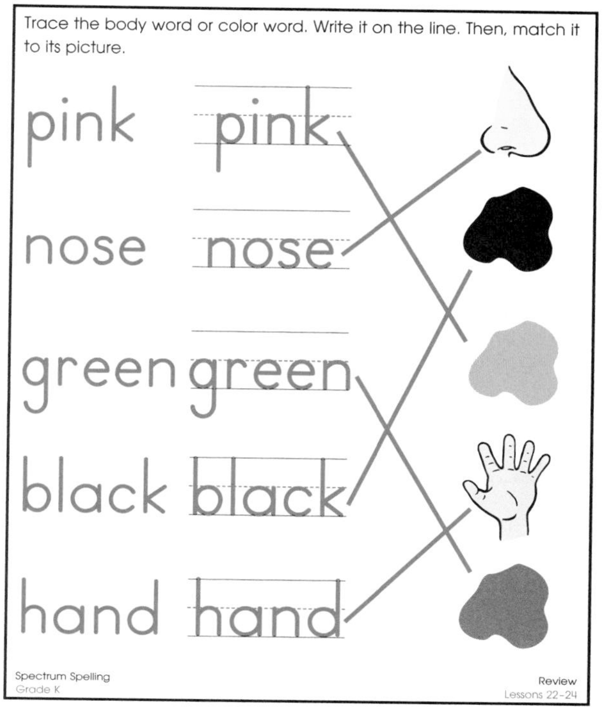
Trace the body word or color word. Write it on the line. Then, match it to its picture.

Spectrum Spelling
Grade K

Review
Lessons 22–24

87

Fill in the missing letters in the food words. Use the words in the box to help you.

apple	juice	milk	bread	peas	soup

Spectrum Spelling
Grade K

Lesson 25
Food Words

88

Draw a line from each word to the food it matches.

Spectrum Spelling
Grade K

Lesson 25
Food Words

89

Answer Key

Fill in the missing letters in the school words. Use the words in the box to help you.

pen paper book desk write read

pen

paper

book

desk

write

read

Spectrum Spelling
Grade K

Lesson 26
School Words

90

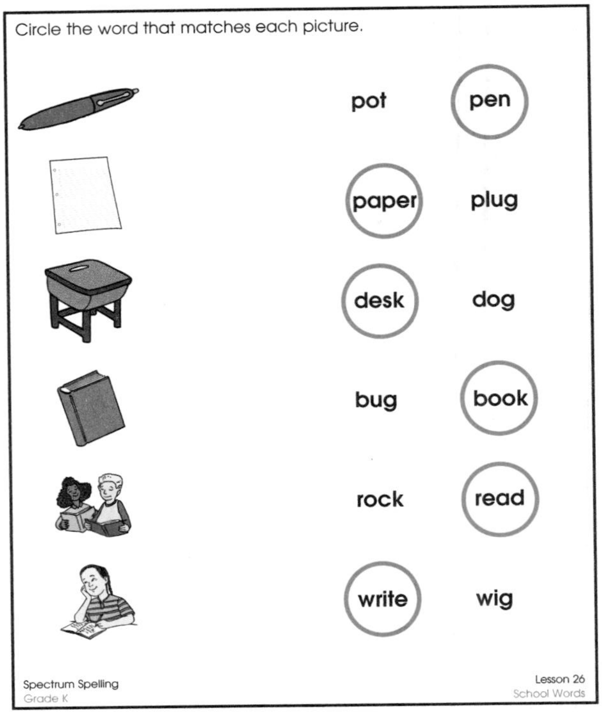
Circle the word that matches each picture.

pot **pen**

paper plug

desk dog

bug **book**

rock **read**

write wig

Spectrum Spelling
Grade K

Lesson 26
School Words

91

Trace the name of each season. Write it on the line. Then, color the picture.

spring
spring

summer
summer

autumn
autumn

winter
winter

Spectrum Spelling
Grade K

Lesson 27
Season Words

92

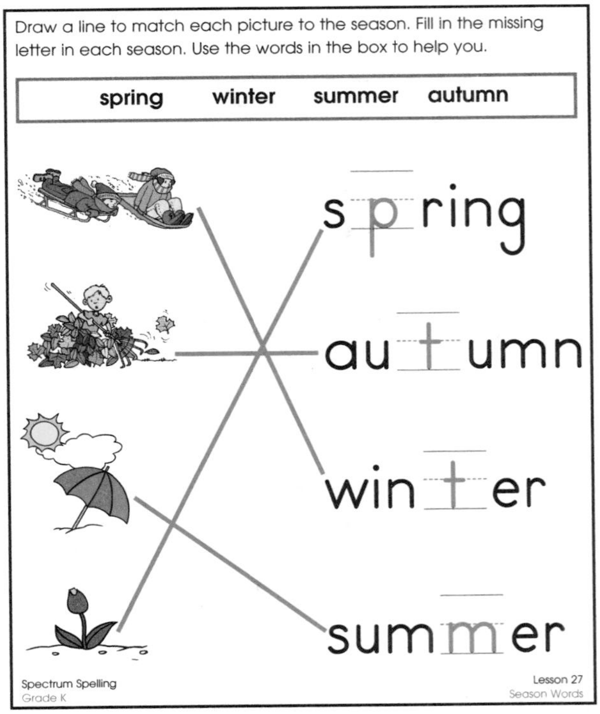
Draw a line to match each picture to the season. Fill in the missing letter in each season. Use the words in the box to help you.

spring winter summer autumn

spring

autumn

winter

summer

Spectrum Spelling
Grade K

Lesson 27
Season Words

93

Answer Key

Choose a season from the box. Draw a picture of that season. Write the season word on the line.

spring winter summer autumn

Answers will vary.

Label should match drawing.

Spectrum Spelling
Grade K

Review
Lessons 25–27

94

The letters in the food words are in the wrong order. Say each picture name. Then, write the correct word on the line.

sopu soup

mikl milk

pepla apple

The letters in the school words are in the wrong order. Say each picture name. Then, write the correct word on the line.

nep pen

boko book

dear read

Spectrum Spelling
Grade K

Review
Lessons 25–27

95

Use this page to practice writing some words that tell about you.

What is your name?

How old are you?

What Answers will vary.

Do you have a pet?

What is its name?

Spectrum Spelling
Grade K

Writing Practic

97

Notes

Notes

Notes